Early Childhood Education and Sustainable World

C000240844

Making an important contribution to the growing body of literature addressing the issue of sustainability in the Early Years, Sandra Smidt provides a highly accessible text examining the philosophical, political, economic, social and cultural aspects of sustainability impacting on very young children today. Drawing on current and global research, Smidt presents case studies and vignettes illustrating good practice and positive thinking in this constantly expanding field.

After clarifying the myriad of acronyms used in this subject area, the book turns to the question of defining sustainability, before chapters explore a diverse range of topics:

- How very young children make sense of the world and the critical role of teachers and practitioners in listening and responding to the questions they ask.
- The young child as a citizen with a voice that needs to be heard, and ideas and opinions which should be shared.
- Examples of how practitioners and settings are working democratically in recognition of the intellectual capacities of young children.
- Possible pedagogies to support the learning and the emotional needs of very young children in relation to issues of sustainability.
- The integration of services offering Early Childhood Care, and those offering Early Childhood Education.
- Analysis of the professional standing of early childhood educators.

Other key issues addressed in the text include the worldwide impact of global warming, globalisation, capitalism and human aspiration. Smidt expertly navigates these issues, illustrating good practice and providing those working with young children with the knowledge and understanding they need to support children to develop, maintain and live in a sustainable world.

Sandra Smidt is a writer in early years education.

Early Childhood Education and Care for a Shared Sustainable World

People, Planet and Profits

Sandra Smidt

Routledge
Taylor & Francis Group

LONDON AND NEW YORK

First published 2019
by Routledge
2 Park Square, Milton Park, Abingdon, Oxon OX14 4RN

and by Routledge
711 Third Avenue, New York, NY 10017

Routledge is an imprint of the Taylor & Francis Group, an informa business

© 2019 Sandra Smidt

British Library Cataloguing in Publication Data
A catalogue record for this book is available from the British Library

Library of Congress Cataloging in Publication Data
Names: Smidt, Sandra, 1943- author.
Title: Early childhood education and care for a shared sustainable world : people, planet and profits / Sandra Smidt.
Description: Abingdon, Oxon ; New York, NY : Routledge, 2019. | Includes bibliographical references and index.
Identifiers: LCCN 2018013023 (print) | LCCN 2018028033 (ebook) | ISBN 9781351068963 (eb) | ISBN 9781138478312 (hbk) | ISBN 9781138478329 (pbk) | ISBN 9781351068963 (ebk)
Subjects: LCSH: Early childhood education--Study and teaching--Case studies. | Sustainability--Study and teaching (Early childhood)--Case studies. | Sustainable development--Study and teaching (Early childhood)--Case studies. | Environmental education--Study and teaching (Early childhood)--Case studies.
Classification: LCC LB1139.23 (ebook) | LCC LB1139.23 .S643 2019 (print) | DDC 372.2107--dc23
LC record available at https://lccn.loc.gov/2018013023

ISBN: 978-1-138-47831-2 (hbk)
ISBN: 978-1-138-47832-9 (pbk)
ISBN: 978-1-351-06896-3 (ebk)

Typeset in Bembo
by Servis Filmsetting Ltd, Stockport, Cheshire

Printed and bound by CPI Group (UK) Ltd, Croydon, CR0 4YY

This book is dedicated to all the wonderful early childhood practitioners, teachers and carers, thinkers and writers, researchers and students whose footsteps I hope to stand in. And – of course – to the children whose questions sometimes take our breath away.

Contents

Preface

Writing a book for those working with very young children on how to develop, maintain and live in a sustainable world might seem an odd thing to do, but it does not take too much thought about the state of our world as we start the year 2018 to recognise that we, as a species, have lived our lives paying scant attention to the damage our values, actions and consumerism have done and continue to do to our precious world. In the past two years we have witnessed terrible acts of war, terrorism and genocide; storms of extraordinary power devastating homes and crops, killing the old and the young; people leaving their homes because their crops have failed, there is no work, no food, no place for them; mass migration across oceans and deserts, mountains and plains; people leaving their simple homes and land and moving to cities in search of something better. All of these people include millions of young children. This is their reality. They are the ones whose future is so threatened.

I have been writing books on early childhood for more than a decade and know that even very young children think deeply about what happens to them and their friends and family. Even when they hear about dreadful things happening to children whom they do not know, they understand and feel for what is happening to these strangers. Those who live or work with young children might initially find it difficult to know how to talk to them about their fears and concerns and many childcare workers, parents and teachers regard sustainability as being 'too difficult' and the children 'too young'.

But perhaps you remember the Zeebrugge ferry disaster nearly 40 years ago. At that time I was working with young children in a school in Stoke Newington. They had seen the disaster take place on television. Many had been on ferries with their families, going on holidays to France. They were bursting to talk or write or draw or act what they were feeling and fearing. They raised questions, developed their opinions on why and how it had happened; they considered what they might have done if they had been there. One child could not believe that water could be heavy enough to sink a ferry full of heavy vehicles. Another child said 'If it ever happens to us my mum PROMISES she'll be saved first. I wouldn't want to be alive without my mum.'

In this book I want to hold fast to my faith in both children being serious and competent and aware of all that happens to and around them and adults who work or live with them sharing this belief and creating situations where children are invited to ask questions, express their feelings, consider implications and get answers. This, for me, is meaningful engagement in real and important issues.

My thanks go to Michael Rosen for allowing me to use his poem in this book.

Introduction to the book

Education for sustainable development is a relatively new field of study, only now becoming a truly global movement. This book is aimed at all those interested in, caring for and educating young children. The realities of how the natural, physical, political, social and educational worlds have changed and are still changing are evident and affect not only us but our children and grandchildren. They see and hear things that they may not understand and look to us to help them. In order for us to be able to do this there are two questions to be answered: what do we understand by sustainable development and what is its significance for our young citizens?

I like to use illustrative case studies and try to ensure that these are drawn from both the developed and developing worlds. You won't be surprised to learn that it is sometimes difficult to find case studies from many of the developing countries.

As in all my books I use 'she' rather than 'he' to talk about the generic child and embedded in the chapters are sections where I invite you to make an assessment or evaluation of something in the text.

The layperson's guide to acronyms and icons

CK	Campus Kindergarten
DAP	Developmentally Appropriate Practices
ECD	Early Childhood Development
ECEC	Early Childhood Education and Care
ECE	Early Childhood Education
ECCE	Early Childhood Care and Education
ECEfS	Early Childhood Education for Sustainability
ECECfSSW	Early Childhood Education and Care for a Shared Sustainable World
ECRP	Early Childhood Research & Practice
EfS	Education for Sustainability
ESD	Education for Sustainable Development
FAO	Food and Agricultural Organisation
GPI	Genuine Progress Indicator
GDP	Gross Domestic Produce
NGO	Non Governmental Organisation
OECD	Organisation for Economic Cooperation and Development
OMEP	*Organisation Mondiale pour L'education Prescolaire* (World Organisation for Preschool Education)
SD	Sustainable Development
SDGs	Sustainable Development Goals
UN	United Nations
UNESCO	UNESCO is responsible for coordinating international cooperation in education, science, culture and communication
UNICEF	United Nations International Children's Emergency Fund
UNROC	United Nations Convention on the Rights of the Child
7Rs	reduce, reuse, recycle, respect, repair, reflect and refuse.

 You will see this logo each time we ask you to think about something. The figure on the left is the Arabic symbol for a question mark and the one on the right is used in a range of European languages.

Chapter 1

Defining sustainable development

Key words and concepts: defining sustainability; the concept of sustainability; achieving sustainability; global perspective; need to change our behaviour; concept of needs; competing needs; idea of limitations on meeting needs; three pillars of sustainability; investing in the early years; children's rights and capacities.

Defining sustainable development

Defining sustainable development is much more difficult than you might have thought at first glance. To do this one needs to think across boundaries of subject matter and consider a wide range of issues. Weldemariam *et al.* (2017) say that sustainability is '*a discipline that requires major efforts to ensure the well-being of people and planet now and in the future*' (2017: 2) This is a straightforward enough definition and the words in it that strike me as essential are *major efforts, well-being, people, planet, now* and *future.* They remind us that if sustainability is to be real it must refer to the urgent need for the human race to act quickly and do whatever is possible to protect people and this world we live in. There is an emphasis on making the solution not for the short term but forever.

The most commonly quoted definition of sustainability is that of Brundtland (1987), which states that '*Sustainable development is development that meets the needs of the present without compromising the needs of future generations to meet their own needs.*' It contains within it two key concepts: a) <u>the concept of needs</u> – in particular the essential needs of the world's poor, to which overriding priority should be given, and b) <u>the idea of limitations imposed</u> by the current state of technology and social organisation on the environment's ability to meet present and future needs.

There are many other attempts to define sustainability, and the only other one I want to cite is that of Schumacher: '*Development does not start with goods; it starts with people and their education, organisation and discipline. Without these three, all resources remain latent, untapped, potential.*' You can find this in his first book – a collection of essays that has the wonderful title *Small Is Beautiful: A Study of Economics as if People Mattered* (1973: 138). This book brought his ideas to a wider audience just as an energy crisis was shaking the world and people had started to recognise that petroleum and other natural resources are finite (that is, such resources should be treated as nonrenewable capital rather than as expendable income, to be exploited and used up without thought for the future). Schumacher was a Rhodes Scholar and a highly regarded economist who worked with key thinkers like J.M. Keynes and J.K. Galbraith. He developed an early interest in 'sustainable development' and opposed neo-classical economics by declaring that a single-minded concentration on what he called output and technology was dehumanising. He also wrote that one's workplace should be first dignified and meaningful and only efficient after that.

It was while travelling in Burma in 1955 that he first talked of 'Buddhist economics', which was based on the notion that good work is essential for proper human development and that '*production from local resources for local needs is the most rational way of economic life*' (Haughton and Hunter 2004: 62), He also looked at globalisation and its effects, and wrote that:

> *Ever bigger machines, entailing ever bigger concentrations of economic power and exerting ever greater violence against the environment, do not represent progress: they are a denial of wisdom. Wisdom demands a new orientation of science and technology towards the organic, the gentle, the non-violent, the elegant and beautiful.*
>
> (in Moss 2008: 265)

It is my intention that this book mirror the approach of Schumacher in terms of addressing what we, who have created the global crisis, must do to educate the next generations to make changes so that they have a world in which life and learning can be sustained.

Sustainability as a critical global issue

It was at the end of the 1980s that the Organisation for Economic Cooperation and Development (OECD) published the *Brundtland* report in which, for the first time, the concept of sustainable development as a critical global issue was mentioned. It was then that the role of education for global survival was born. And since then there has been a widespread recognition that sustainability is a serious issue for all countries and people, not only for today but for the future. To address it a global perspective, involving both individuals and groups, needs to be taken. In order for sustainability to be effective, economic, social and environmental conditions and processes need to be integrated into a whole. Sustainable development is, of course, about how things change and it is evident that some change can be negative. Those most likely to be affected by sustainable development are the youngest in our world so the consideration of developing early years education for sustainable development is perceived by many educators, researchers and others as an essential current topic for consideration.

In answer to the question of what sustainable development is, it has been suggested that in order to deliver sustainable development there is the need to focus on three pillars. These are the social, the environment and the economic or, as some people would have it, people, planet and profits – sometimes called the three Ps.

*   The <u>socio-cultural pillar</u> is often less visible and less considered than the other pillars. In order for the planet to remain viable, those living on it need to be able to be in paid work, under acceptable conditions. They must be entitled to have a voice so that they are actively involved in the decisions made about things that impact on their lives and will impact on their children's futures. These include the things that we all rely on – such as safety at the workplace; fair employment conditions; decent and safe homes; and access to quality education for ourselves and our children.

People also need to have a voice in local affairs and be accepted by their society where their languages and cultures need to be valued. In other words they must gain or retain the right to be full citizens.

- The <u>environmental pillar</u> is the one most of us are familiar with. It is focused on saving the environment with an emphasis on thinking about nature and the effects of global warming. Most of us know something about the impact on the planet of our carbon footprints – the damage we all do through the practices of our daily lives such as the disposal of waste, water usage, burning coal and dumping of plastic in the seas. Sadly there are still those who insist on continuing to cut down trees, dig mines, frack rocks, build unnecessary railways and pollute waterways, all in the face of undeniable evidence of the negative impacts of what we are doing. Here we encounter for the first time the over-riding consideration of 'profit rather than planet'. There are, of course, some places where things are slowly changing as the growing body of in-your-face-evidence of harm and damage grows. But change is slow and businesses and governments are often difficult to persuade to change their procedures.
- The <u>economic pillar</u> relates mainly to business and issues around profit and loss and the policies of governments (local and other) or other bodies that are in control of the money for funding things like hospitals, education, care, social housing and safety precautions. We have been witness to what can happen when rules governing safety are ignored, as in the tragic fire at Grenfell Tower in London in 2017. Business plays a very dominant role in the developed and, crucially, the developing world. Many capitalist countries take very seriously the needs of business and the reality is that for a business to survive it must be profitable. In many places the needs of business rule and across the world it seems that greed still trumps need. The economic pillar with regard to sustainability requires that there is proper governance, and that risk assessment and social needs are taken account of.

It is the inclusion of the economic pillar and profit that makes it possible for corporations to come on board with sustainability strategies. But the sad reality is that business may stand in the way of sustainability since for many the needs, or rather the desires, of the rich are considered at the expense of the real needs of the poor.

 This is your first question. What factors can you identify in today's world that you believe are causing negative changes which are damaging the well-being of people and the planet?

You will almost certainly mention climate change but did you think of any or all of the following?

- pollution;
- drought and wasting water;
- lack of planning with sustainability in mind;
- use of fossil fuels;
- effects of the intense growth of cities;
- loss of farming;
- cutting down of trees and forests;

- the impact of technology and the Internet;
- the power of corporations, business, selling and advertising;
- the role of social media.

Considering globalisation

Globalisation is the process by which the world has and is becoming increasingly intercon-
nected as a result of massively increased trade and cultural exchange. It is commonplace
now for people to relocate and change countries. This is not, however, a new phenom-
enon and it has been happening since time began. My grandparents, for example, fled the
rise of fascism in Europe; my parents left South Africa because of apartheid. Mass migration
has always been part of the world but it is clear that it is increasing as people are drawn to
the industrialised and rich developed countries as their countries become poorer. People
move for many complex reasons – for a better life, for survival, to be with their extended
families, to flee war or famine or to find paid work. So globalisation can be viewed as
largely positive or as extremely damaging. It all depends on who and where you are.

 Can you think of the positive effects of globalisation on you and your
family, community and culture?

One of the positive effects of globalisation on society is increased diversity in terms of
cultures and language. I see this as an advantage because our culture can only be enriched
by others bringing their cultures into ours. Think about how our diets have changed,
for example. We can choose from all the cuisines of the world in cities like London. We
have access to French films, Italian food, Chinese ceramics, Australian literature, Korean
technology and more. We can learn from those who come here just as they can learn
from us. How much culturally richer this country is than it was when I first arrived here
in the 1960s.

   In terms of how globalisation benefits children in the early years much depends on
the views and attitudes of the adults in their lives. The benefits for young children of
meeting new little people who perhaps look and sound different from them, but behave
just like them and play with them, are obvious. They are all children of the same world
where they will have to share its resources and keep it safe to live in. When, however,
the children encounter the hostility shown by some adults to migrants or refugees –
people different from 'us' – they may experience some cognitive dissonance and find it
difficult to benefit from the diversity. As poor people arrive in their new countries they
often experience the impact of living in a society organised for the benefit of the rich
rather than for all. Capitalism and the idea of making money seem to be essential for an
improved quality of life. There is an overwhelming belief that money brings happiness.
For many coming to the UK the two things that many of them say they want more than
anything is to have more money and to speak English – both of which are seen as the
doors to a better life.

   In 2005 the World Bank Report announced that they were going to intervene and
invest in early childhood education. Here is the report of their findings in 2017.

> *Investing in the early years is one of the smartest things a country can do to eliminate extreme
> poverty, boost shared prosperity, and create the human capital needed for economies to diversify*

and grow. Early childhood experiences have a profound impact on brain development – affecting learning, health, behaviour and ultimately, income. An increasingly digital economy places even greater premiums on the ability to reason, continually learn, effectively communicate and collaborate. Those who lack these skills will be left further behind.

Yet today, millions of young children are not reaching their full potential because inadequate nutrition, a lack of early stimulation, learning, and nurturing care, and exposure to stress adversely affect their development.

The challenge is daunting:

- *In low and middle income countries across the world, 250 million children under the age of five are at risk of not reaching their developmental potential because of poverty and stunting (or low height for age).*
- *In Africa alone, one third of children are stunted.*
- *Worldwide, only half of all three to six-year-olds have access to pre-primary education. In low income countries, just one in five children has access to preschool.*
- *One in 200 children in the world is displaced, exposing them to the kind of stress that can undermine their development.*
- *Investments in young children are minimal: in Sub-Saharan Africa just 2 percent of the education budget goes to pre-primary education, while in Latin America government spending on children under 5 is a third of that for children 6 to 11.*

Smart investments in the physical, cognitive, linguistic, and socio-emotional development of young children – from before birth until they transition to primary school – are critical to put them on the path to greater prosperity, and to help countries be more productive and compete more successfully in a rapidly changing global economy.

There is a growing body of evidence about what programs work: early childhood nutrition, early stimulation and learning programs to extend school completion, all improve learning outcomes, and ultimately increase adult wages. Some of the evidence includes:

- *A 20-year study of children in Jamaica by Nobel laureate James Heckman, Paul Gertler and others showed that early stimulation interventions for infants and toddlers increased their future earnings by 25 percent – equivalent to adults who grew up in wealthier households.*
- *A World Bank Group (WBG) analysis of the long-term benefits of early childhood education in 12 countries found that children who attend preschool stay in school for nearly a year longer, on average, and are more likely to be employed in high-skilled jobs.*
- *Children in a long-term study in Guatemala who were not stunted were much more likely to escape poverty as adults, and earned incomes 5 to 50 percent higher than children who were stunted as children.*
- *Evidence that an additional dollar invested in quality early childhood programs yields a return of between $6 dollars and $17 dollars.*

(World Bank 2017; last updated: 24 October 2017; www.worldbank.org/ en/topic/earlychildhooddevelopment)

The statistics provided in this brief article are shocking. We know that poverty is the biggest danger we face and of course young children who have access to care and education will flourish. But do you see providing early childhood education and care as a purely generous gesture? I fear that many will see it largely as a good business venture and when this happens we are in the market place. We are not only concerned for the well-being of the children but we get caught up in a philosophy that ensures that those with money will get the best and the rest of us will get what is left over. What has happened is that corporations and manufacturers in the early childhood world are vying with one another to 'sell' their offer and in this way education itself has become a valuable resource in the knowledge societies of today.

 Do you think that making a profit out of the things that damage the physical and natural worlds – like poisons or practices – is justifiable?

To answer this question you need to think about the competing needs that operate. On one hand there are the rich and powerful people thinking only about themselves and the here and now, and holding enough power, money or influence to totally ignore the views and needs of the poor, with not only less money but also with little or no influence or power. For me the most important issue related to sustainable development, is the consideration of the balance of different and often competing needs against an awareness of the environment, which means not only the natural or physical environment but also, crucially, the social and economic structures.

 Read this and reflect on what you learn from it.

Slash and burn is an endemic agricultural cropping practice in the tropical rain forest regions of western Africa, South America, and southeast Asia (Kotto-Same et al. 2000). The practice consists of cutting down trees on part of the forest to clear space for an agricultural plot. After allowing the cleared foliage to dry, the farmer then burns the downed trees and immediately crops the land. Two to four years later, the farmer moves to new areas as agricultural yields on the cleared plot fall as a result of weeds, insect pests, plant diseases, and declining soil fertility.

(cited in Nganje, Schuck, Yantio, and Aquach 2001)

 Now read this and say what you learned from it.

The Food and Agricultural Organization of the United Nations (FAO) estimated that between 1981 and 1990, the average global deforestation rate in the humid tropics was 0.1 to 0.14 million-km² per year, resulting in millions of hectares of degraded land, increased production of greenhouse gases and major loss of biodiversity (FAO, 1985). In Cameroon, about 100,000 hectares of closed canopy forest is lost annually, taking the estimated rate of deforestation to 0.6% (FAO, 1997). Kotto-Same et al. (2000) also attributed some of the problems of low productivity and food security to slash and burn cropping systems. FAO (1985) pointed out that under conditions of rapid population growth, slash and burn as a cropping system has relatively weak potential to provide rural populations either with adequate food supplies or sufficient income to support healthy and prosperous lives. On the

whole, slash and burn agriculture leads to environmental degradation, low food production, and overall food insecurity in tropical rain forests.

(Nganje *et al.* 2001: iv)

This small example highlights just how a practice, developed years ago, continues despite the fact that its effects contribute to increasing poverty and food insecurity as well as damaging the environment itself. Nobody can suggest that the farmers are acting out of greed: they are clearly just applying what they learned from their fathers and forefathers. This is a case of lack of up-to-date knowledge about our world.

 Who is responsible for the continuation of practices like these?

Let's now think about the continuing use of fossil fuels as a primary source of energy and how this impacts on our world. You will know that fossil fuels are rock-like, gas or liquid resources that are burned to generate power. They include coal, natural gas and oil, and are used as an energy source in the electricity and transportation sectors. They're also a leading source of the world's global warming pollution. We pay for them in our energy bills but have no real appreciation of the cost they have for our world and our future. We can see some of the external effects of these fuels such as pollution and land degradation. We may experience effects on our own bodies like becoming asthmatic or developing cancer. And those living close to the sea may notice the rise of the sea level. Many consequences are far removed from our daily lives and may only affect a minority or marginalised subset of the population. But there are costs in terms of money, health, long-term changes and more. It is difficult to ascribe our dependence on fossil fuels to ignorance or custom. We well know the effects and ignore them because it suits us in the developed world to drive our cars and heat our swimming pools, and put coals on our barbecues. But at what cost? The choices that have been made by businesses, governments, banks and rulers have been largely made for the benefit of the haves and to the detriment of others. Development throughout much of the world can be said to be driven by the current needs or desires of particular groups without considering the possible or wider impact on others. It is a totally imbalanced system. For development to be sustainable there needs to be a balance between the desires and needs and will of one group concerned with how things are at the time and another group looking to the future, and do this against an awareness of the environment and of the social and economic limitations that we all face as a society.

Achieving sustainability

So what do we need to do to achieve sustainable development? We need to devise a set of realisable goals and work towards these. I suggest our goals might be as follows:

* A recognition of the competing needs against an awareness of the physical, economic and social worlds.
* The maintenance and preservation of the environment.
* Knowing and meeting the diverse needs of all people in existing communities and for the communities in the future.

- Promotion of personal well-being, social cohesion and inclusion.
- The creation and maintenance of equality of opportunity.

You will find more about the sustainability goals of the United Nations in Chapter 5.

 Do you think that children in the early years need to be concerned with sustainable development?

This simple question is more complex than it seems. If we think about how many settings for early childhood have an outdoor play area or a garden or are set in the forests or take the children on nature walks, the answer is a simple 'yes'. But one of the most important things to note is that educating children for sustainability is about much more than teaching them to care for the natural world. In the words of Amartya Sen, a Nobel prizewinner and economist, to educate young children about sustainability we have to go beyond that to ensure that we regard each child as having agency and the ability to change things. In short, we educators have to teach children to '*think, assess, evaluate, resolve, inspire, agitate, and through these means reshape the world*' (2000: 2).

 Do you think Sen was correct?

I do and that is because this is how I see all human beings, however old or young – all as having agency and continually asking questions in order to come to understand the world and the people and objects and events in it. There are millions of very young children throughout world and what happens to the world impacts on them and on their development. In the very recent past we have read and heard of horrific hurricanes, earthquakes, droughts, floods and wars, all making children suffer hunger, homelessness, pain, fear, isolation, being wounded or orphaned. The only thing to reassure us is that we live in an age when we can take for granted that children have rights, enshrined in the United Nations Convention on the Rights of the Child (UNICEF 1989).

Child development and sustainability

Margaret Chan, the director of the World Health Authority, wrote a piece in *The Lancet* (2013) called 'Linking child survival and child development for health, equity, and sustainable development'. It is essential reading.

   She starts by charting the successes in child health over the years but then asks if the surviving children will have an equal chance of realising their human potential, living in a world where there is social justice and contributing to sustainable development. In effect she is questioning whether the children of today will have the opportunities and chances of previous generations and the same opportunities as their peers. She tells us that there are three areas which form the basis for healthy child development, and these are:

- stable, responsive, and nurturing caregiving with opportunities to learn;
- safe, supportive physical environments;
- and appropriate nutrition.

She is a doctor with in-depth understanding of what are best practices in terms of health and physical thriving.

Three areas are critical foundations for healthy child development: stable, responsive, and nurturing caregiving with opportunities to learn; safe, supportive, physical environments; and appropriate nutrition. These foundations include many familiar best practices: planned, safe pregnancy and childbirth; exclusive breastfeeding in the first 6 months of life with appropriate complementary feeding and responsive feeding; preventive interventions such as vaccines for the treatment of infections and diseases; and protection from toxins, violence, and other environmental hazards.

A stable and engaged family environment in which parents show interest and encourage their child's development and learning is the most important of these foundations. Such supportive human relationships promote and protect a child's physical and mental health, behaviour, and learning across his or her lifetime.

(Chan 2013: 1515)

This is very straightforward and obvious and relevant because there is much said and written about the consequences of a small child's life being hijacked by life experiences caused by poverty, stress, reduced access to support services and more. Chan reminds us that we must try to ensure that children develop on a heathy pathway because we know the damaging effects of neglect, deprivation of love or nutrition, being chastised, ignored, required to adopt adult roles and maltreatment. She ends her piece with these words:

Promoting healthy child development is an investment in a country's future workforce and capacity to thrive economically and as a society. By ensuring that all children have the best first chance in life, we can help individuals and their communities to realise their maximum potential, thereby expanding equality and opportunity for all. As world leaders are preparing the post 2015 development agenda, the time is right to recognise that investment in early child development is essential, not only for good health but also for sustainable development.

(Chan 2013: 1515)

Children's rights and capacities

Julie Davis is Associate Professor in Early Childhood Education at Queensland University of Technology in Australia and co-editor with Sue Elliott of *Research in Early Childhood Education for Sustainability*. In the opening chapter of the book Davis and Elliott describe how the work arose out of the presentations and discussions during two transnational conferences on early childhood education for sustainability – one held in Stavanger, Norway (2010) and the other in Brisbane, Australia (2011). The authors contributing to the book – which arose from the conferences – adopted a child-centred approach, with the young child as thinker, problem solver and agent for change. This is very much the stance we take in this book. Davis came to the conclusion that she needed to examine and revise children's rights in light of what is happening to the world. Her work is important in that it makes us all consider what rights even very young children have or should have as active citizens. The rights she developed are as follows:

•   foundational rights refer to the rights of the child to develop and survive; be protected from abuse, neglect, exploitation and cruelty. They are the rights to be kept safe.

- <u>participative rights</u> are the rights to be listened to and heard and to be active in society.
- <u>agentic participation rights</u> reflect the twenty-first century views of the young child as being able to make sense of her world and her place in it; to share her thoughts and ideas; to have insights and perspectives that help adults better understand what she feels and thinks. This right is closest to what Sen (mentioned earlier) was talking about.
- <u>collective rights</u> – as members of groups children have not only individual rights but also rights related to the groups to which they belong.
- <u>intergenerational rights</u> – very young children are involved with those older and younger than them and develop a concern for their peers, their parents, their siblings, their grandparents and generations to come.
- <u>biocentric/ecocentric rights</u> – the words biocentric and ecocentric mean the same: that all forms of life matter.

The philosophical basis for this book is that children, from birth, seek to understand this world and the people and objects in it. They live with other people in social groups and through their interactions with others come to make and share meaning. Those living or working with young children and sharing this view of the active, questioning young citizen will listen attentively and respond appropriately. They are the logical candidates to learn about how to ensure a sustainable world for their futures.

Moving on . . .

This introductory chapter sets the scene for thinking more about sustainability. In the next chapter we look at the questioning child and the listening adults.

Chapter 2

The questioning child:
the listening adult

Key words and concepts: competent meaning-making child; listening attentive adult; preverbal communication; born into a social world; interpreting what is seen and heard; no curriculum; teaching and learning; child's perspective; dialogical teaching.

In this chapter the primary concern is to reveal the young child, from birth, being social, interactive, communicative, intent on becoming a member of her family, culture and community and engaged in trying to understand the world and the people and objects in it. This is no helpless creature but one asking questions and finding answers in order to actively engage with the world. <u>Every person who encounters this child must view her as questioning and competent.</u>

In this chapter we also examine the role of the teachers or other adults or more expert others who are interacting with the child and <u>asking if they are really listening to the child, hearing what the child says and paying attention in order to understand what problem she is trying to solve or question have answered.</u>

 Read what follows and say if you think this is a questioning child.

Penguins in Antarctica

This example comes from a city nursery for children aged between 3 and 4 in New Zealand where Glynne Mackey was carrying out some research to determine the child's right to participate in action for the environment. She gave this account, which serves as an excellent example of how determined young children are to make sense of their world.

> *Several children gathered with their teacher, around a calendar of Antarctica. During a conversation about penguins in Antarctica, a young child expressed his concern for baby penguins that might die in the extreme cold. This child moved to the side of the group and began to invent his own three-dimensional penguin-saving device using a plastic construction set made up of various lengths and shapes of plastic that could be connected with nuts and bolts. He initiated a detailed conversation with me about how this device would solve the problem of penguins dying. He proudly showed his teacher and the children listened intently as he demonstrated how his 'machine' would work.*
> *Child: This machine can actually save the penguins.*

Teacher: Oh look.
Child: The baby penguins.
Teacher: Oh, I'd like to hear about that, Liam. Tell me how it saves the penguins.
Child: You use it when it is very snowy. It can land on the sea and it can land on the ice. It's all right if one bit falls off because you can put it back together again.

(Mackey 2012: 479)

I hope this leaves you in no doubt that this little boy is asking questions, expressing his ideas and his feelings, inventing a solution to the thing that he is questioning. He is an ordinary little boy who has been invited to voice his thoughts and act on them.

He, like his peers, is a questioning and competent child.

Wendy Scott, writing in Cathy Nutbrown, gives us another questioning child – this time 5-year-old Sonnyboy who is a traveller child just starting school, who asks the teacher *'Why do you keep asking the kids questions when you know all the answers? Like . . . like what colour is it then? You can see for yourself it's red . . . so why do you keep asking them?'* (1996: 36). Here is a child trying to make sense of something that makes no sense yet is often still common – teachers asking questions instead of responding to the questions implied by the actions or gestures or words of the children.

 Read the example below and ask if you think this is a listening teacher.

Sigridur Aadnegard and Gestny Kolbeinsdottir wrote a chapter about a preschool in Blonduos, a small town in the north of Iceland, where there is a prawn processing plant right in the residential area. The plant often gives off foul fumes, which explains the title of the chapter – 'The prawn stench'. The position of the plant and the fumes it gives off cause conflicts of interest in the town since many workers are dependent on the plant for their livelihoods. The teachers in the preschool heard some of the children talking about the smell and also about how they loved prawn salad. The teachers in this case started the project by putting the children into different roles to try to understand different points of view about the presence of the prawn stench. Two of the children played at being the owners of the plant and another two children played at being people living close to the plant and being very badly affected by the smell. Here is an extract of the dialogue between children and teacher.

Child: You have to stop processing prawns, the smell is so bad.
Child: We can't do that, because then people won't get food and they'll die.
Teacher: What do you think about that? What can you do?
Child: We'll just move.
Teacher: Don't you think it might be possible to find another solution? Perhaps no one wants to buy the houses you live in.
Child: They'll just have to hold their noses when they go out.
Teacher: But what if they have their windows open; then they're going to have to hold their noses for a very long time.
Child: They just don't open any windows; they just stay inside and take it easy.
Child: But then we can't go out to buy food.

(Appendix to Norddahl in Pramling Samuelsson & Kaga 2008: 78)

The teachers in this example were clearly listening to the children since the project was based on what the children were interested in and concerned about and the interventions made by the teacher did, to some extent, allow the children to keep the dialogue going.

Becoming a questioning child

How the human infant becomes a competent and questioning child is something to marvel at. After 9 months in the womb the infant emerges ready to interact with others and become part of a family, a community and a culture. It is through her interactions with others that she comes to understand her world. Where she lives is often significant in terms of her life chances. And whom she lives and interacts with is also significant in determining many aspects of her future. We will touch on the roles of significant adults in the child's life first in terms of how the child's actions, gestures, expressions and vocalisations enable that adult – usually a parent – to take seriously what it is that the child needs or wants to know more about. Parents very often see their young child as being communicative and will often talk of just how brilliant their baby is. The truth is that it is not only one baby who is brilliant but almost all babies as long as they are taken seriously. When the child starts going to an early childhood setting she may come into contact with some adults who still think of young children as being not *yet* competent. Too often young children are not recognised as being thoughtful and questioning and yet the evidence shows that they are. In essence we are talking of the questioning child and the interpretive and supportive adult. With babies the communicative cycle goes like this:

> Giulio is 10 months old and being fed at a table by his mother. He wants his digger. He <u>looks intently</u> at it and <u>makes an almost pointing gesture</u> in its direction.
> Then, significantly, he <u>looks directly at his mother.</u>
> <u>His mother reads the signal, gets the digger and is rewarded by a large grin.</u>

Not yet verbal but effectively using all his means of communication to shape a request. He was not asking a question in this case but asking for assistance. Giulio's mother was, like almost all mothers, a listening adult (personal observation notes).

 Would you agree that this is the reverse model of traditional schooling where the teacher asks questions for the child to answer?

Early learning and development

We know from the work of people like Colwyn Trevarthen that it is from the moment of birth that the human infant seeks interaction with her mother or other primary caregiver. The infant not only responds but sometimes initiates an exchange. What is happening is that

> *from birth, the human infant together with the primary caregiver is able to establish a social collaboration based on how they express their feelings by adapting expressive movement, gesture and the sounds of their languages and culture. This allows them to establish what Gratier and Trevarthen (2008) call intimate connectedness. The early interactions of mother and baby allow*

the two to build a way of knowing one another within their own world, their own culture. For the infant language, the meanings of words or 'semantics', can play little part in this. She does, of course, hear the sounds and words of the language used by the mother, and she recognises rhythms and tones, but it is through the combined synchronous activity of gestures, vocalisations, expressions and feelings that she begins to contribute to and share and understand the knowledge and values of her culture. This intimate connectedness places her within her social and cultural group before she can talk.

(Smidt 2018: 28)

So the human infant is born into a social world of people who have developed particular ways of operating. With every interaction the infant is paying attention and indicating by gesture, facial expression, sounds and actions the need to learn to find out more. She is seeking to make sense of everything and everyone she encounters. You may have noticed a baby looking attentively at something she wants or pointing at something that interests her or making a sound she has not made previously. Before she acquires spoken language she is already communicating. Living in a social world she is not only making meaning but also, and crucially, sharing meaning. She is raising questions about her world. At nursery or creche she will be asking questions just as she does at home but the questions will not be always spoken. Identifying communicative behaviour and interpreting it correctly is one of the things early years professionals become good at. It is exactly what is meant by the questioning child and the listening adult. When working or living with young children it is essential to be aware of just how hard they work at both making sense of this world and contributing to it. Trevarthen again tells us that the human infant is born almost pre-programmed to become an active member of her family and community. The word active is important.

We know that there is little or no doubt that a young child who witnesses the effects of an earthquake or a flood, or who has to leave her home and becomes separated from her family, or is hungry every day because there is not enough food, asks questions. Any child experiencing such terrible events must ask existential questions such 'Why?', 'Why me?', 'How?', 'What now?', 'How can we stop it?', 'Where do we go?', 'Who can help us?' Very young children may not verbalise these questions but their facial expressions, body language and actions tell us of how they are needing to make sense of the tragic events engulfing their world. I worked with young children for years and found the questions they raised pertinent, individual, significant and always needing answers. Sadly, some adults involved with children tend to want children to answer their questions rather than be helped to find answers to their questions.

There are, of course, many adults who immediately recognise and respond to the urgency of the questions raised by the children, whether these are spoken or implied. One of the most significant in the world of early childhood is Vivian Gussin Paley who was a very significant figure in my early years of teaching and who recognised that in order to be a good teacher of young children she needed to listen to them. She became a kindergarten teacher in the United States and at first did what she was asked to do until the day a high school science teacher asked if he could spend time with the young children in the kindergarten. He had a grandchild about to enter nursery school and he wanted to know how to teach such young children. He very quickly established an amazing rapport with the children and Paley noticed that he talked to the children and listened to them and, most importantly, was truly curious to hear their ideas and thoughts. Paley realised that what he was doing that made him a model was to be genuinely interested in what the children were saying and that was the starting point for all that followed. From that day Paley turned her classroom into a place where the children determined what to do. She abandoned using any set curriculum, handing the decisions about what would happen each day to the children. Sadly, many educators and those who set the terms for their training and work are more interested in scores and league tables than they are in what the children are thinking.

 Does the idea of having no curriculum excite or terrify you? Read on to see how Paley was not alone in her courage.

Teaching and learning

Teaching young children is not, or should not be, all about teaching them how to read and write, count and measure, colour in neatly or sit quietly on the carpet and put up their hand to answer a question. It is about seeing children and hearing them – paying attention to what they are concerned about, interested in, frightened of or even celebrating. Small children live in the real world which, for many, is a hard place to be. To be a good teacher or a fine carer or a true educator, you must know the children you teach and know about the worlds in which they live. Then, through looking and listening, you might have a chance of offering different ways in which they can deal with their feelings, their fears, and the realities they face.

Many years ago I was delighted to be invited to visit the famous nursery schools in Reggio Emilia started by Loris Malaguzzi. Their approach to early education and care was singular and exciting. Walking through the nurseries it was immediately apparent in all the rooms that it was the children who were determining what was happening. It was there that I began to appreciate how vital it is to really listen to children, hear what they say and respond appropriately.

 Read these real observation notes and then say what you think the child was asking or interested in or paying attention to.

- *Samu and Giorgio are playing with the blocks when they see a bug. Samu says 'It's not moving. Look it's not moving any part of its body.'*
- *Giorgio says 'I don't like it. It could sting me even with my pants still on.'*
- *Oliver tries to sweep up the bug using the small brush and shovel from the sand tray. He taps the bug and listens to the sound the tapping makes.*

(Smidt 2013: 48)

These are the sorts of conversation you might hear in any early years setting. There is nothing special about them. They become more significant if you try to analyse each in terms of what you think the child is interested in, questioning or discovering.

This is my analysis:

- Samu is wondering if the unmoving bug is dead. I have noticed that some very young children are interested in what it means to be dead and you may encounter children asking questions about death itself.

- Giorgio seems nervous about being stung and fears that this might happen despite him wearing trousers. Perhaps he has been stung in the past and remembers the pain.
- Oliver realises that the others are not keen to have the bug close to them so he finds a way to move the bug and then, interestingly, taps on its shell and listens to the sound it makes. Perhaps he is asking what the shell is made of, if it is hard or not and what purpose it serves. Interestingly his actions show his ability to empathise with the anxieties or dislikes of others.

And here are two vignettes when it is what the children *do* rather than what they *say* that gives us a window into their thinking.

- *Alessi peers into the puddle, seeing his reflection. He walks round and round, looking down all the time. He climbs onto a step and looks down from a greater height. He pulls Giorgio to stand beside him and they both look into the reflection.*
- *Livia spots a trail of ants going across the path. She watches intently and gasps when one of the ants picks up a very large breadcrumb. Another ant comes over to help carry. She watches for a long time.*

(Smidt 2013: 64)

 Here are some rather more complex and well-hidden questions being raised by the children's behaviour rather than words. Find the question or questions being asked by each of the children.

In my analysis below you will see that I have put the words that tell me how the children were communicating without using words in bold:

Alessi **walked** round the pond and **looked** down on it from the steps. He was using his actions to express the questions he was asking. Perhaps he was asking if his shadow moved with him.

Livia **gasped** when she saw a small ant lift a large breadcrumb. Her amazement is apparent and her question obvious.

The children in the provision in Reggio Emilia are assumed to be learning all the time although there is no set curriculum being followed. The underpinning philosophy is that all young children actively do their best to make sense of every event, object or person they encounter and do this through the interactions they have with significant others. So learning is taking place everywhere and through everything that happens. The observed interests or concerns of the children determine what the children do. The roles of the adults are to know the children, pay attention to what they do and say, respond appropriately and think about how to provide opportunities and resources so that the children can explore ideas, make things, express their feelings, verbalise their ideas and needs and ask for help when needed. They learn primarily through play – choosing for themselves what to do and how to do it.

 Do you think that very young children need to be 'taught' formally?

The very word 'taught' makes me think of something that is imposed on children. And where there is a set curriculum it is evident that someone, somewhere has decided what all children falling into an arbitrary age group and wherever they are, should have learned by some point in time. Sommer, Pramling Samuelsson, and Hundeide (2013) explain their preference for what they call a *child perspective paradigm* – one that links care with education – and explain the origins of their thinking as follows:

> *With a basis in the UN Convention on the Rights of the Child (1989), which has been ratified by 192 countries, a rationale is introduced that spells out and draws attention to the implications of giving young children a voice, having responsibilities, listening to them, and trusting them as competent individuals. When children's own experiences, world views and actions are recognised as fundamental to early care and learning, a specific child-oriented paradigm will be needed.*
>
> (2013: 4)

Initially I was rather confused by the authors of this piece making a distinction between child perspectives and children's perspective. However, on reading on, my confusion was resolved by reading this:

1. *Child perspective(s) means that the adult's attention is directed towards an understanding of children's perceptions, experiences, utterances and actions in the world. Thus a child perspective is not the child's experience. This means that, despite the ambition to get as close as possible to children's experiential world, a child perspective will always represent an adult approximation.*
2. *Children's perspective(s) represents children's own experiences, perceptions and under-standings of their life world. In contrast to the child perspective, the focus here is on the child's phenomenology as a subject in their own world. That is what adults strive to understand through their child perspective approach.*

(Sommer *et al.* 2013: 7)

The authors list five basic assumptions underpinning a child perspective-oriented approach. For them the best practice is where the adult and child interact and communicate on the basis of the adult seeking to know what the child is asking, interested in and concerned about.

Seeing the child as a person. It really goes without saying that anyone working with children should see the child as a person to be respected, included, loved and influenced by others. She is not an object but a person who can enable other children and adults to empathise with her and to join in. In essence it requires the adult to try and stand in the child's shoes.

Empathic participation with the child. To empathise is to feel for another or, as the authors say '*seeing the child's face*'. I would add that it requires also hearing the child's voice, noticing her expressions and gestures and actions and understanding what she is paying attention to. It means also to follow the child's lead, provide emotional support and establish contact and trust. In this way the adult and child establish a secure relationship of what the authors call reciprocal-attachment. The positive implications for mental health are obvious.

An interpretative attitude of respecting the child's utterances and world of meaning. This refers to what has been dealt with earlier in the chapter namely the ability and willingness to be an attentive listener and interpreter of communicative signs.

Guiding the child in a sensitive way by adjusting and expanding their initiatives. This refers to what Bruner called scaffolding (Wood, Bruner & Ross 1976), which means being focused on what it is that the child is trying to do and offering help to enable the child to succeed. It has links also to Rogoff's guided participation (1990), which is rooted in involving the child in reallife tasks alongside more experienced others. The authors go on to tell us that '*There is, of course, an educational goal set by adults – a goal that is not necessarily the child's goal, but which has to be negotiated in the dialogue.*' I wonder what you think of this.

Early care and education is a dialogical process between the child and the carer/ teacher, where both contribute to the learning objective – sometimes the teacher is dominant, at other times the child. Dialogic teaching is something that interests me so do read on to see if it also interests you.

Dialogic teaching is an interesting approach to learning and teaching. Jayne White, author of *Introducing Dialogic Pedagogy: Provocations for the Early Years* (2016) was influenced by Mikhail Bakhtin who was best known in the field of literary theory. When the research focus in education switched from the image of the abstract, individual child to the active, contextualised, social child whose competencies are interwoven with the competencies of others, the work of Mikhail Bakhtin (1895–1975) became known and, in some places, popular. He was a contemporary of Vygotsky and his concept of 'dialogical meaning-making' states that the learner plays an *active role* in developing a *personally constructed understanding* of the *curriculum* through a process of *dialogic interchange*. The curriculum in this sense refers to what the child has chosen to explore. In dialogic pedagogy different opinions and ideas are considered; there is a respect for the views of others and a collaborative approach to what is done.

 Read through these two case studies and then ask if you see them as examples of dialogic pedagogy or practice.

Case Study 1: Musim Stream Project in Korea (for 5-year-old pupils)

What the children said or did to spark things off

A child said 'My mother said there were many otters in Musim Stream before, but now they are gone.'

Another child responded saying 'I have never seen an otter in Musim Stream. Are otters still living in the stream? What do they look like? '

How the adults responded

They showed the children some video clips of otters on the Internet and brought in a booklet about their city. Someone from the community was invited in to tell the children that otters were still living in the stream. The children continued to be interested in the fate of the otters.

How the children dealt with what they had learned

They asked more and more questions, such as 'Where do otters live now? How do otters build their houses? Do otters eat only fish and no cookies?'

The project went on and on with the children drawing pictures, making clay models, writing letters to express their love of and fear for the fate of otters, visiting otters in the zoo and making books.

What I loved most about this project

A letter to an otter which goes '*Dear otter, I hope you have many babies and live happily in clean water. I really want to see you but don't come out of the water. Don't get caught by the hunters.*'

(Okjong Ji and Sharon Stuhmcke in Davis and Elliott (eds) 2014: 164–166)

Case Study 2: The birds are bored: Reggio Emilia 2011

What a child said to spark things off

Four-year-old Luigi looked at the birds outside the window and said they looked_bored because they had nothing to do and nothing to do things with – no toys or play equipment.

What the adult did in response

She listened carefully, took notes and began to think about where to take this. She recognised that Luigi has expressed a concern about something he had noticed and interpreted this as the child empathising with the birds and internally both raising and answering questions about why this might be so. A situation pregnant with the potential for much learning – and not only for Luigi. She invited Luigi to tell his friends what he was thinking about and they set about considering what they could make to keep the birds entertained. The teacher listened and recorded what they were saying.

How the project developed

The children were in a nursery in Reggio Emilia and projects like this were and still are everyday happenings. They visited a local playground, taking drawing materials with them to draw the play equipment. On their return they went out into the garden to choose a possible site for their bird playground. They began to design and draw the things they would make – swings, slides, a roundabout, a climbing frame, a bench to perch on. They asked the teacher to make a list of what materials they might need. They then set about making the things they had designed and then placed them outdoors and watched to see how the birds responded.

What I loved most about this project

The fact that the children were concerned about the happiness of the birds: they cared about them. It is close in theme of concern for others to like the children worried about the otters.

The right to know

Back in New Zealand Glynne Mackey's children are still asking questions, engaging in conversation, solving problems and making decisions as they go. Here are some more of their delightful questions, ideas, solutions, discoveries, evaluations and theories.

> *Adult: What bowl do you put the food in for the worms?*
> *Child: I think this one*
> *Adult: Oh, OK. And what sort of food do they like?*
> *Child: They eat bread but not meat. Did you know that worms are vegetarian?*
> *Adult: Are they?*
> *Child: Yes,'cause they don't like eating . . . they don't like to eat meat stuff like that.*
> *Adult: Oh. OK. Why do they like eating paper?*
> *Child: Because . . . it's because it's good for them and they just like eating it sometimes.*
>
> (Mackey 2012: 478)

> *One morning in the kindergarten, one of the children communicated his empathy to care for the natural world by cradling a dead monarch butterfly carefully in his hands. This child often struggled to develop a positive relationship with his peers yet they gathered around him to share his concern and empathy. His teachers affirmed his actions, trusting that in caring for the natural world he would be more likely to build caring relationships with his peers and others.*
>
> (Mackey 2012: 479)

Moving on . . .

In this chapter you encountered young learners and found out something about how eager and intent they are on understanding the world and the people and objects in it. They are continually asking questions, verbally or through looking, gesture and movement. You have also encountered the adults in their world who really pay attention to what the child is asking or interested in. In the next chapter you start to look at young learners as citizens in their own rights.

Chapter 3

The child as citizen

Key words and concepts: children's rights to education and to care; adults in waiting? neoliberalism; consumers; early childhood in the free market; capitalism; becoming a citizen; being a citizen; forming a collective; taking responsibility; construct new rights.

In this chapter we look at how children are viewed both in the developed world and in the developing world and ask if how we see our young children reflects the rights assigned to them by the United Nations.

Children and their rights

In much of the world young children have *a right to education and care*. In their earliest years as babies and toddlers they may well be cared for and educated at home or in home-like settings by parents, grandparents, siblings, childminders or other paid or unpaid people. In developed countries and some developing countries, where the parents are working or decide that it would be good for the child to meet other children, parents or carers may choose to send the child to a playgroup or creche or other early years facility. Later still the child might be sent to a nursery school or join a nursery class in a school. Often nursery classes are attached to primary schools and mainly government funded. Throughout the world there are many choices and parents will choose according to their needs, values and pockets. When the child reaches what is regarded as school age in her country of residence, she enters what is regarded as formal education. Before that, mothers or primary caregivers who work part or full time may be able to send their young child or children to a playgroup, take the child with them to the workplace if that is acceptable, attend a creche attached to the mother's workplace and, finally, on reaching the age of starting school, enrol them in a nursery class of the nearest school. It all hinges on what is available and/or affordable and accessible and appropriate.

Whatever provision the parents or carers choose, it is important to remember that young children have rights. They have the *right to be protected from harm, abuse, neglect and exploitation* and the *right to be heard and be active in their homes and beyond*. In addition to these individual rights they also have *rights according to the groups with which they are involved*. The rights of children with disabilities, or the rights of immigrant children or the rights of children in hospital are examples of group rights. In most of the developed world it is the norm for young children to be part of some government sponsored provision in the form of early years education/care and although this will vary from country to country, early years provision is increasingly becoming privatised as businesses see money-making possibilities and exploit them. As a business rather than an entitlement, the prevailing goal of such settings is to make money rather than to care for and educate children. Little attention may be paid to understanding the learning or emotional needs of young children and how to meet them. The nurseries may look smart and be well resourced in terms of furniture and play equipment, but evidence suggests that they may not view the child as being competent, independent, social and a person in her own right. Rather, they tend to see the young child as incomplete and needing intervention and remediation to allow her to become a thinking, questioning, engaged being in her own right. As a consequence there are providers who offer early years care and/or education based on the concept of early years education being nothing but preparation for adulthood. Do remember this when you come to Mike Rosen's poem, which you will find later in the book.

 When you think of the young children you know, do you think of them as being like 'adults-in-waiting' or as small people working hard alongside others, trying to make sense of their world?

It is easy and relatively common to think of the small child as incomplete. In certain academic disciplines (psychology and sociology perhaps), the image of the young child is that of someone weak and needy rather than active and competent; with needs rather than rights. It is important to know that the image of the child is a cultural and hence a political construct. A construct is a set of ideas that come together to stand for something significant. We have made the *young child* a construct, which means we can, if we choose, see it differently – namely seeing the young child as having competence, values, intelligence and potential. Young children are not waiting to become full people in the future but are current citizens in a culture that needs to recognise their potential. Young as they are, they have ideas and values and need to have a voice that is heard. Many live in consumerist societies dominated by the values and roles and rules of businesses, manufacturers, corporations, companies and advertisers eager to grab their attention – and their money. In recent years the privatisation of early years settings has become commonplace so that early childhood education and care is now firmly out in the market place. There is a lot of money that can be spent by rich parents on education, books, toys and equipment all under the notion that what you pay for is more valuable and 'better' for your child.

Neoliberalism and the creeping effects of the corporatisation of childcare

In their writing about early childhood education in Australia, Woodrow and Press (2007) talk of *the corporatisation of childcare*. They were obviously writing about early childhood in Australia but what they say is applicable to much of the developed world. Here, as in Australia, a wide variety of childcare is on now on offer and where it used to be more of a community service it is now something to be chosen, purchased and paid for by parents. It's like buying a coat or a hat or a holiday. It is important to think carefully about the implications of this for our children and their future. Many practitioners, writers and researchers agree that the privatisation of some nursery education, with its view of the child waiting to become an adult, may have damaging consequences for the child. One danger is that each child involved in such a setting becomes a self interested individual, knowing something about what the most desirable objects to possess are, but little about her companions and their interests and fears. In all likelihood she constructs her self image through desiring, acquiring and competing. In fact she herself has become a victim of consumerism. Evidence of this comes from the work of Cribb and Ball (2005), who tell us that privatisation does not simply change the way we do things but also changes what we *think* about ourselves and about others. When the child goes to a private early years setting the parents become consumers who remain largely passive in the sense that the only decision they need to make is that initial choice of which nursery – i.e. the product. We know that as consumers children and adults are influenced by advertising and marketing, and become subject to the vagaries of the market place. In turn the corporate childcare business has no true educated interest in the quality of what it is selling. For them the issues which concern us in this book – those relating to sustainable development – will not feature in their thinking or planning.

Neoliberalism is the term used to describe the free market capitalism which emerged in the twentieth century and which is illustrated by things that will be familiarto you – austerity and deregulation. It means keeping the rich rich and the poorpoorby not even attempting to redress the huge divides which define capitalist societies.

So neoliberalism is not new and nor is its relation to early childhood. What happens is that early childhood provision is seen as a business with one setting competing with another on the basis of which is 'doing better'. The question of what 'better' in this context means remains. Along with this is the extension of practices drawn from the world of business to assigning some number to suggest where the setting sits on some mythical scale measuring 'quality'.

The problem with 'quality'

Many people talk about assessing the <u>quality</u> of early childhood provision but there is a huge problem in coming to any agreement about what quality might look like. Dahlberg, Moss and Pence said of quality that it

> *cannot be conceptualised to accommodate complexity, values, diversity, subjectivity, multiple perspectives and other features of a world understood to be both uncertain and diverse. The 'problem with quality' cannot be addressed by struggling to reconstruct the concept in ways it was never intended to go.*

(2007: 105)

To speak of quality in regard to early childhood provision fails to recognise the realities of this world of ours, which is *multilingual* and *multicultural* and *multilayered* and *complex*. To talk of quality is to use the language of the market place not of early childhood provision. If we are thinking of how to evaluate provision we have to take time to seriously consider the process as involving democratic interpretation which involves making practice *evident* so that those involved can reflect on, discuss, argue and agree so that their judgement can be challenged and not set in stone. How you can make evaluations or judgements means recording and examining in detail what each child or group of children have done, said, made, constructed, contributed to, changed or shared.

For the young child the possible consequence of becoming a consumer-in-waiting is how she comes to see the world at large. She lives in a world full of shiny and desirable things which are possibly available if she sheds a tear or two, or nags and pesters until she is successful. Alternatively she might become unhappy because she sees that her peers have things that are newer, shinier, bigger, faster, louder. But it does not have to be like that. In the provision in Reggio Emilia and nurseries and kinder-gartens in Norway and Sweden, in Australia and even in the UK, everyone is assumed to be there to learn and to learn from one another – adults and children, teachers and care staff. Nothing is forbidden as long as no one is hurt. The day is full of things to look at or do, touch or smell. You may use a mirror or a magnifying glass, lie down and look at the sky or crawl on the grass outside. You can run and skip, plant something, pick up an ant, paint a picture, shake a tambourine, make a model, ask for help, cry if you are sad, laugh if you are happy. It is your world in the here and now, where you are living your life and learning about life, not a preparation for something to come. As you come to make sense of it all, alongside others, you are learning about how and why things happen; how to get help when you need it; different and similar; same and different; me and you.

Neither seen nor heard?

Being a citizen implies having the right to speak and be heard; to belong and be recognised. In law, however, being a citizen is complex and I am not going to go into detail about the arguments about whether or not children, particularly in the early years, can be regarded as citizens. Elizabeth Cohen (2005) has written a paper called 'Neither Seen Nor Heard: Children's Citizenship in Contemporary Democracies' – a wonderful title which sums up the problems posed when those with power regard young children as being nothing more than adults in waiting. Yet young children can hold passports; in developing countries many may work; some are put in the role of acting as the head of the family and certainly think and express their thoughts when listened to.

Sue Nichols argues that young children, waiting to be recognised as citizens are not sitting silent and unmoving but participating in communities where they already are or would like to be. Through their acute observations of how groups work they know that being a member or belonging is better than being an outsider. More than that they have worked out how best to become a member. The adults may be in charge of the space, and of how it is used, but the young children in the study seeks to be a part of it. Each child wants a voice and rights; to be heard and taken notice of. She wants to know who is powerful and why and how this came about. There are clearly rules and customs or practices about how the children should behave in any setting. For example, in class can they talk whenever they have something to say or must they put up a hand? Can they look at a book whenever they want to? Can they throw the food on their plate on the floor? Nichols talks of the *five Ls* rule, which means '*lips locked, legs crossed, hand in laps and looking at the teacher*'. How repressive! I imagine that you have encountered something similar in your lives. She argues that what children do is form their own collectives and here is a tiny example. Please note that the significant features in this vignette are underlined.

It is <u>*free drawing time*</u> *in the reception class. Rose is sitting at a table with* <u>*five other girls.*</u>

Various girls:	*I can follow you.*
	You can follow me.
	We can follow each other.
	Then I'll have it after you.
	Hey, let's do that cool thing again.
Rose:	*Can I too?*
Girl:	*We all are.*
Alicia to Rose:	*You have to copy me OK? I'm putting stars on my picture.*
Rose:	*Me too.*

Rose writes near the top of her page.

            I like to see bu.
            I like to see bi (then she stops).
Lucy: <u>*We don't usually write when we just draw.*</u>

The teacher had established this activity session as one where children were free to draw whatever they wished; the use of 'free' in this context signals, through its unvoiced opposition, the 'unfree' nature of most school activities. The mixing of linguistic and visual texts had not been banned or even discouraged by the teacher. The girls had, however, worked to produce an institutionalised 'unfree' version of the activity of drawing through the injunction to 'follow', the use of the collective 'we' and the policing of the boundaries between visual and linguistic texts.

(Nichols 2007: 123–124)

I remember well when my older daughter Andy came home from her first day in a nursery class and complained bitterly, saying:

She said I had to put up my hand every time I wanted to ask a question. I want to ask lots of questions all the time. I just went to the toilet and she was cross with me for not asking. Then I went into the book corner to look at the books and she said it wasn't reading time. When we could go in the garden she wouldn't let me go until I put a hat on and I didn't need a hat. It wasn't raining.

(personal notes)

That was a very long time ago and Andy never stopped asking questions and later challenging things that made no sense to her. In essence she was acting like a little citizen but without any power to change things.

Project Zero

Looking online for case studies of young children acting as citizens I came across 'Project Zero', a link between early childhood provision in the United States and Reggio Emilia. Being very familiar with the philosophy of Reggio Emilia I went online and found an engrossing and highly entertaining video about a project about the Boston Marathon. The video is called *Learning Is a Team Sport* and you can find it on vimeo. com 21372133 https://vimeo.com/21372133. I laughed in delight so do try to find it. The case study below also comes from Boston and shows how, when children are treated as citizens in the sense of being both seen and heard, they reveal their complex thinking about their world. In finding out about the world they live in and the people they interact with, young children can be seen and heard addressing what we might call the big issues.

 Below are three examples for you to read and consider. What evidence do you find in these of children behaving like citizens? And what evidence can you find of other people regarding young children as citizens?

Case Study 3: A fairer and more interesting place for children: Boston, Mass. (2014)

The background

The children in this example are used to working in the way they do in Reggio Emilia where they often go out into their cities and towns to look and talk or draw and make. On their return they are able to work individually or collaboratively asking questions, making suggestions, sometimes drawing or making.

How the project began

In this case it was the intervention of the mayor of Boston who started the whole project by writing a letter to all the early years settings in the city inviting them to tell him what *new things they thought should be built in their city to make it a fairer and more interesting place for children.* Since this request is likely to be relevant to the children and something where they can draw on their expertise they are more expert on this matter than the adults.

How the adults responded

The staff in the nursery schools are used to working on the basis of listening to the children and responding appropriately. They listened to what the children were saying and recorded what they heard – namely the thoughts and ideas of the children. The adults provided them with the resources to make things and wrote down what the children said they thought that the city's children, like them, would enjoy having. Since the children were not yet writing with ease, the adults wrote the words to be sent to the mayor.

What the children decided and did

The mayor had addressed the children as citizens and asked them to perform a civic act of considering the needs of all the children in their community. The children responded as citizens. For example:

- At Leticia Nieves' Tobin School the children made a book of their ideas, which included the following: a dragon fountain, a dinosaur museum, mountains, a park to walk cats, better roads and a flower garden.

- At Harvard Kent, ideas for Boston included: *kids' toy cars in Boston that children can drive to school by themselves, a new park for kids with more flowers and more trees, a lot of new Boston toy shops for children and bouncing houses in the parks for Boston children.*
- At Blackstone School, children wrote books about how to make Boston fairer and more interesting. Ideas included: *more helpers, more bridges, candy and maps, ways to keep kids safe, more toys for kids so they will be happy and smarter, and a machine that makes food so no one will be hungry.*
- At Ellis School they decided that children need more exercise so they built a model of an *indoor playground to be used in winter. The playground had a sandbox, swings and a running track. The playground has a roof with solar panels.*
- At Curley School they decided to make one big place where all the suggestions of interesting places for children would be in one location. So they created a *Water Travel World with a zoo, park, aquarium and pool. You had to arrive by boat so there needed to be a parking lot with a walkway to the boat launch.*

Case Study 4: Making a How to . . . book: Providence, Mass. (2015, 2017)

The mayor of Providence, which is also in Massachusetts and involved with Project Zero, also believed that it was important to involve young children as citizens in issues about democracy and decision making. A letter was sent to all early years providers inviting the children to make a book about something they could do well and knew a lot about. The request was to make a 'How to . . .' book explaining carefully how you do something. The children could write about how to ride a bike, how to bake a cake, how to water the plants, how to pick up a worm or about anything else they could do. They were urged to take their time in making their book and it was suggested that they get advice and help from teachers, parents and friends. The letter ended with these words: *Work hard on your books since many people will see them. There are plans to display your books at the Providence Children's Museum and our public libraries . . . a few of us adults want to make a 'how to' book too . . .* (Krechevsky, Mardell, & Romans, 2015).

I love the fact that Leah, one of the children, made a book called **How to Whistle**!

Case Study 5: Young architects?

Lillgården's preschool in Sweden was old, and a new preschool was to be built on an adjacent area to it. The architect invited the children to get involved in designing their new out-door space. Here is what Siraj-Blatchford **et al.** wrote about what followed:

They realised that there were different heights, and secret places they wanted to save, places where they could grow flowers and vegetable, where they could have construction work, barbecue etc. They asked: 'Is there room for the old apple trees, or can we plant new ones?' 'Can we grow tomatoes somewhere?' 'Can we make a small pond where the birds can drink and we can play?'

(2013: 9–10)

This was followed by a phase when the children began to use what they knew about the old playground and where

> they began to apply all of their experiences and knowledge about the old area of the preschool, transferring it into new maps and new signs. Some of the old signs still worked, but they also had to invent new ones. They made a map with signs, and also a model with suggestions for the new playground. For the model they used cardboard, paper, cloths, paint, etc. The model construction of the new preschool playground was exhibited for parents and for the municipality who were responsible for the new building and playground facilities. Also the local newspaper came and took pictures and a debate started in the community about the role of children as active citizens. Economics also become a question since the children themselves posed many of the questions about what they wanted in the new playground. It depends on how much money one has!
>
> (2013: 10)

It is evident from these three small case studies that young children want to belong to a community for many reasons, one of which is so that they can be heard. They are thinkers, asking questions implicitly or verbally, so that when they are listened to they give evidence of how social and political they are. Three important names in the world of those working for EDS in the early years are John Siraj-Blatchford, Kimberly Caroline Smith and Ingrid Pramling Samuelsson. They have been active in the field for many years and have organised and contributed to conferences and written papers. Their book entitled *Education for Sustainable Development in the Early Years* published under the umbrella of OMEP is available online at www.worldomep.org/wp-content/uploads/2013/12/combined_ESD_book.pdf. The booklet is easy to read and understand and apart from restating the arguments about the significance of educating young children to build and live and learn in a sustainable world, it has case studies of things that young children and their teachers and carers around the world have done – all illustrated by line drawings by Anna-Karin Engberg. This case study comes from this book.

Meet Carlina Rinaldi: Adelaide Thinker in Residence (2012–2013)

Carlina Rinaldi, incomparable early childhood thinker, teacher philosopher, and advocate for young children went from Italy to work in Australia for a year as thinker in residence. What a wonderful title and an amazing opportunity! Influenced by Loris Malaguzzi and her colleagues she brought with her the image of the child I think all human beings should hold. I am going to paraphrase some of it. If you want to look at the document itself you can find it online at https://www.education.sa.gov.au/sites/g/files/net691/f/reimagining-childhood.pdf. What you will find is a beautifully presented document full of Rinaldi's thoughts and those of Malaguzzi as well as some children's work.

I went to Reggio Emilia several times and met both Rinaldi and Malaguzzi as well as their colleagues. I visited provision there and in other Italian towns and brought back ideas that continue to influence me. Their work has been very influential and is funded well, which partly accounts for its success. Many people throughout the world have been influenced by their philosophy and their practice but it is sometimes the case that what has been borrowed or copied is the look rather than the deep intentions of Malaguzzi and his colleagues. As you already know, I share Rinaldi's image of the child as being cultural and social and political. All children live with others, are part of a culture and hold a position in their society. The way in which many people think about young children may be as being dependent, needy, inexperienced, small and weak versions of adult. Yet we know that, from birth, the human infant is actively making meaning, sharing meaning, joining in, looking, listening, moving, reaching, pointing and essentially sociable. It is evident that what we believe about young children becomes a significant factor in determining their social and ethical identity, their rights and the educational and life context offered to them. Rinaldi says that

> Our image in Reggio Emilia, part of our theory, views children as strong, powerful and rich in potential and resources, right from the moment of birth.
> As Loris Malaguzzi wrote, it is the image of the child who, from the moment of birth, is so engaged in developing a relationship with the world, and intent on experiencing the world that he or she develops a complex system of abilities, learning strategies and ways of organising relationships.
> In this sense, we share the values and meaning of the constructivist and social constructivist approaches. We see a child who is driven by the enormous energy potential of a hundred billion neurons, and by the incredible curiosity that makes the child search for reasons for everything, and who has all the strength and potential that comes from the ability to wonder and to be amazed. A child who is powerful from the moment of birth because of being open to the world, and capable of constructing his or her own knowledge.

> (2013: 15)

It is important to read on because Rinaldi's passionate description of their image of the child is so detailed and so essential to understanding the ways in which they work and which might well influence your thinking about early education, particularly in regard to sustainability.

> Our image is of a child who possesses his or her own directions and the desire for knowledge and for life. A competent child!
> Competent in relating and interacting with a deep respect for others and accepting of conflict and error. A child who is competent in constructing; in constructing his or herself while constructing the world, and who is in return constructed by the world. Competent in constructing theories to interpret reality and in formulating hypotheses and metaphors as possibilities for understanding reality.
> A child who has his/her own values and is adept at building relationships of solidarity. A child who is always open to that which is new and different. A possessor and builder of future, not only because children are the future but because they constantly re-interpret reality and continuously give it new meanings.
> Our image is of the child as a possessor and constructor of rights, who demands to be respected and valued for his/her identity, uniqueness and difference. To think of a child as a possessor of rights means not only recognising the rights that the society gives to children, but also creating a context of 'listening' in the fullest sense. This means that we must recognise and accept the uniqueness and subjectivity of each human being (and thus each child), as well as create spaces that are self-generative, that is, spaces where each child can create and construct new rights.

> (2013: 160)

Read the closing sentence below and say what you think it is telling us.

A society which 're-cognises' (re-knows, re-understands) its childhood adds not just a social subject but modifies itself because, in recognising children's rights, it recognises new rights for everyone.

(Rinaldi 2013: 16)

My interpretation is that where a society is able to take what children do seriously it becomes a society which recognises that they have rights. All children are working to make sense of the world by doing, examining, making, trying again and this is serious work. They have earned the right to have rights.

Now meet Susan Isaacs

Having just read some of the thoughts of a modern practitioner, researcher and writer, you are invited to go back more than a century to discover Susan Isaacs. Recognising how clearly young children think about their world is not something new. If you have not come across the work of Susan Isaacs you have missed a treat. An extremely brilliant and some would suggest a Renaissance woman, she studied biology at Cambridge and was, in her lifetime, a child psychologist, philosopher, free thinker, writer, psychoanalyst and an educator of young children, their parents and their teachers. I first came across her work as an undergraduate at Wits University in Johannesburg when my aunt gave me a hardback copy of Isaacs' book *Intellectual Growth in Young Children* published in 1938 and by Routledge. My copy is so well used that it is falling apart and its pages are yellowing and frayed. It is a treasured possession. The book was written almost a hundred years ago and when I first read it I had no real interest in young children but something about how Isaacs viewed them and valued their thinking grabbed my attention. Isaacs was writing about 78 years ago and no one then was even remotely concerned about the sustainability of the planet. But when Isaacs set up the Maltings House School – one of the progressive schools being set up at the time by other liberal thinkers – she said she wanted to map the natural development of children's understanding. She was widely read and a scientist at heart with a keenness to document what she saw and heard. More than that she was eager to analyse what she saw and heard. And what she saw and heard made her believe that young children, at play, following their own passions or interests, were competent, social makers and sharers of meaning. Like Rinaldi, Isaacs regarded each child, however young, as being a competent child. The children were mostly observed by her when they were following their own interests rather than any prescribed curriculum. They were learning through play. She famously wrote: '*Play is indeed the child's work, and the means whereby he grows and develops*' (Isaacs, 1929: 9). This is not something startlingly revealing now but it certainly was then and it is sad that her clear thinking and scientific view is possibly no longer fashionable. There is a profound message in her philosophy and this is that children don't need a top-down curriculum in order to learn. They can make their own curriculum. In much of early childhood provision we often seek to grade young children rather than notice and build on what they can do and what they are interested in. We want our young children to listen and complete tasks that can be assessed in order to grade them like peas.

Isaacs not only wanted to map the natural development of the children but also recognised the importance of children having access to nature – growing things, looking after living things, exploring with water and sand; noticing the sun and rain, trees and flowers, life and death. She approached the children as competent and serious meaning makers and she encouraged them to experiment and use equipment that we might blanch at even considering – things like Bunsen burners and sharp knives for example, as well as making clear that nothing was taboo. Anything could be discussed.

And here, just to make you smile at young children's reasoning, is my favourite quote from Isaacs' book:

> *14.7.25: The rabbit had died in the night. Dan found it and said, 'It's dead – its tummy does not move up and down now.' Paul said, 'My daddy says that if we put it into water, it will get alive again,' Mrs I said 'Shall we do so and see?' They put it in a bath of water. . . . Duncan said 'If it floats it's dead and if it sinks it's alive.'*
>
> (1929: 182)

Later the children decided to bury the rabbit and on the following day talked of digging it up again:

> *15.7.25: . . . They began to dig, but tired of it and ran off to do something else. Later they came back and dug again. Duncan, however, said 'Don't bother – it's gone – it's up in the sky' and gave up digging. Mrs I therefore said 'Shall we see if it's there' and also dug. They found the rabbit and were very interested to see it still there. Duncan said 'Shall we cut its head off?' They re-buried it.*
>
> (1929: 183)

Moving on . . .

In this chapter you considered some wonderful examples of projects where adults took young children really seriously and allowed them to display the rights that they have in law. This is expanded in the next chapter when we look at democracy and politics in the nursery.

Chapter 4

Democracy in early childhood care and education

Key words and concepts: democracy; decision-making; human capital; result is binding; investment; nominate; constitution; rules; anonymous vote; referendum; public life; respect for the environment; evaluate such; challenge a dominant concept; be heard; defend ideas; be curious and uncertain; open to change; critical thinker.

Democracy is commonly defined as government of the people, by the people and for the people. It comes from the Greek – *demos* meaning people and *kratos* meaning power. It is an everyday term but in all the definitions I came across, democracy – the right to vote for your choice – was limited to men and adults. But that was then . . . today in most of the world women have the vote and in early childhood education it is believed that competent and thinking young people's voices should be heard.

 Do you think there are examples of early childhood education and care settings which operate on a democratic basis?

The *Dolli Einstein Haus* in Pinneberg

The best example I found comes from Germany and was cited in *The Guardian* in August 2017 (Oltermann 2017). This nursery offers the children a taste of and for democracy and has been called Germany's first democratic nursery. It has been piloting this experiment for more than three years and there are small tales to tell of how successful it has been. The children are all under 6 years old and are invited to vote on decisions ranging from what to have for breakfast to whose nappy should be changed by which care worker. However when it comes to *when* a nappy might need changing, the adults still decide. From the account it is evident that being able to make decisions and choices is sometimes going to the heads of some of the children. For example, when 6-year-old Pia was told that it was time to go to sleep she responded by saying that the kindergarten's 'constitution' stated that she had the right to decide for herself. The centre lists seven children's rights as follows: the right to sleep; decide what and how much to eat; what to play with; where to sit; voice opinion at any time; who to cuddle with; and who may change my nappy.

The head of the nursery, Ute Rodenwald, and her deputy, Heike Schlüter, both deny that they are modelling the nursery on the non-conformist educational models set up in 1968 – the time of the student movement in Germany. Their defence is that they have a constitution and the children being involved in making decisions means that the nursery has more rules than before the change. The goals are designed to equip the young learners with the skills they will need to survive and thrive in a rapidly changing world. Rodenwald states that 'Democracy is not just about elections. For us it is about people – or children – being taken seriously, and learning to make decisions in a way that doesn't leave other people behind' (Guardian 2017: 104–105).

The nursery operates as it does in response to the needs of most children living in homes where both parents are at work. It is run by non-profit charity Workers Welfare Institution and got its quaint name from the name of a talking bird in a children's book. Children can be registered from their first birthday and the nursery is open from 8 am until 4 pm on weekdays. Voting is just part of life and once a week each group of children meets for a session where they have two rounds of votes. The first is on what topping to have on the afternoon cake and second on what to have for Friday morning breakfast. There are two choices for the cake (lemon or chocolate), which makes this a referendum, and four meal options for the breakfast.

The voting procedure is interesting. The options/choices are in the form of pictures, which are placed where the children can see them. Then, as each child's name is called, she takes a coloured pebble (a *Muckelstein*) and places it underneath the picture of her choice. In both votes the results are first past the post and constitutionally binding – however disgusting the choices are. I love the cited example of pizza and stewed beef with beetroot for breakfast!

The staff are eager to insist that it is up to the adults to learn how to accept children's decisions rather than make demands on voiceless children. When it comes to larger decisions there is a monthly children's council, which is attended by pairs of boys and girls who are regarded as 'passers on'. At one such meeting the staff were taken to task because they had decided to buy a pair of new tricycles without first consulting the children. The children were outraged and told the adults that they had not been authorised to buy the tricycles. Democracy in action!

This wonderful example clearly shows young children having both a voice and/or a vote. This implies some aspect of choice and some degree of agency. We, the people who pay the taxes to fund much early childhood provision, are surely in a position to decide about how our children are to be cared for and educated in the settings that are ours. Reading that extraordinary account of how the young children in the *Dolli Einstein Haus* are being shown respect and, on that basis, are behaving like responsible citizens makes me wish I had had an early educational experience like that. Sadly, I fear that throughout the world, millions of early childhood institutions are thought of as education factories – places where small people do what they are told and what they do is measured to assess their 'abilities'. Allan Luke said of such systems that they were part of an 'internationally rampant vision of schooling, teaching and learning based solely on systemic efficacy at the measurable technical production of human capital' (2005: 12) This is a scathing attack on just how education has become a commodity to be sold in the market place where it is assumed that the 'best' costs the most. When I read the statement from the English Department for Education and Skills/Department for Work and Pensions, 2006 stating that they intended to 'develop in every area a thriving childcare market which will respond to parents' needs for the "delivery through the market"' and how local authorities will have to play an active role in understanding the way the *local childcare market* is working, it made my hair stand on end. There is no mention of learning, of democracy, of pedagogy, of citizenship. Dahlberg and Moss (2005) say that the rationale for the decisions made by successive planners and governments are consumerist and technical. The underlying philosophy is individual choice, competitiveness, certainty and universality. It also makes the false assumption that it is the only way. And just in case you think that something like that is not possible in this country, here is an example to help you think again.

Young children, public spaces and democracy: the BRIC Project (https://www.museums.com.ac.uk/blog/author/nicola-wallis/)

The project was steered by Research Directors from each of the three countries – the United Kingdom, Italy and Sweden. They were: Professor Tim Waller, from the Children and Youth Research Institute at Anglia Ruskin University in the UK; Patrizia Benedetti, from the Progettinfanzia in Bassa Regianna, Reggio Emilia in Italy; and Monica Halborg from Barnpedogogiskt Forum in Gothenburg in Sweden. Six of the most experienced and respected early childhood teachers from each country were given training into research methods, and their colleagues, the parents of the children, local politicians and interested people in the community and, of course, the children, all had a voice in how the project developed.

The project was focused on where the children lived and learned and instead of having occasional days or special outings they went back to the same place over and over again over a prolonged period of time. The first groups to go were children aged 3–4 and the second groups were children aged only 1–2 years of age. Sometimes these places were special places, like the park or a museum or a theatre, but some of the preschools chose places that are more ordinary – perhaps a town square, or just a pavement, or an underpass. Interestingly there was often no planned outcome or activity from the adults – it was simply an opportunity for the children to explore and come to know what became 'their' place.

What these teachers and children did was to record and document each outing using every means at their disposal – so photographs, videos, recordings of what children said, their drawings or models – anything related to the visit. Every four months the preschool teachers would arrange to exchange their findings and thoughts and reflect on what they were learning from their own projects and the experiences of others.

Wallis tells us that the project was based on the desire to move away from the position that young children need to be kept out of public view, safely in their nurseries or kindergartens. The BRIC project is keen to reintegrate young children into the community – their communities – to show that they can be included and considered as competent agents in public life.

 What do you understand about the goal of showing that children are competent agents in public life? And how does this link to sustainability?

The BRIC project's research focused in on two key themes: *community engagement* and *traces*. Community engagement is obvious but traces perhaps needs more explanation. I thought traces might refer to the origins of other people who had been in the place in the past and had left a trace of their visit. But the project had a much more social, cultural and democratic focus. As the project went on, children were spending more and more time in public spaces and their presence became noticed by local people just through seeing the children or watching what they were doing or looking carefully at the marks or signs made by the children, the performances they gave, or the exhibitions they put up. People became interested and started to engage with the children. A fantastic example is the Swedish rail company *Jernhusen*, which, inspired by the preschoolers' regular visits to Gothenburg Central Station, began planning an urban gardening programme which extended to all the stations they managed. Their stated intention was that, from a very young age, children will come to consider train stations as places where communities meet and work together, promoting tolerance and civic involvement through sharing a space.

Many of the children spent time in one of the museums involved in the project – the Fitzwilliam Museum in England, Göteborgs Stadsmuseum in Sweden, and Museo Della Terramara Santa Rosa di Poviglio in Italy. The reaction of the museums involved in the project is interesting because they started to really listen to the children and that made them question their roles in educating young children for a sustainable world. Their document 'Guidelines on Community Engagement: Young Children, Public Spaces and Democracy. Intellectual Output 07' explains their thinking. Wallis says that

> *responding to their 'one hundred languages' as our Reggio Emilia colleagues would say, was paramount. Rather than having set routes and outcomes in mind, the adults followed the children's lead: watching, listening, documenting. Quickly we all realised that we were seeing places anew through the children's eyes. Imagine the power of this in a museum or exhibition context – what might we be missing because of overfamiliarity? Can children help us to make new discoveries about 'our' spaces?*

> (2017: 4–5)

The article ends with these words, which summarise much of what we already know: the provision in Sweden and Reggio Emilia and in parts of Australia is more clearly based on seeing and hearing children as thinkers and meaning makers but there is evidence that the global spread of the English language and neoliberal values is having serious effects on society's image of young children and hence the opportunities provided for them in terms of care and education.

The right of the child to participate in action for the environment

Some of the distinguishing features of early childhood pedagogy could be said to be the following:

- families and communities working together;
- building respectful relationships;
- offering learning that is interdisciplinary;
- taking heed of children's interests, ideas and values;
- adults listening to children;
- children making and sharing meaning and coming together to become a social and cultural hub.

We would find all of these in the provision in Te Whariki in New Zealand, Reggio Emilia in Italy, in much of Australia and the Scandinavian countries and beginning to emerge in South Africa. You will encounter evidence of this in the writing of well-known writers such as Helen Penn, Peter Moss, Sue Elliott, Julie Davis, Glynne Mackey and Pramling Samuelsson and also in the work of three little known lecturers, Vivien Linington, Lorayne Excell and Karin Murris (2011), all at the University of the Witwatersrand in Johannesburg. It is their argument which we will examine here. South Africa, emerging from its history of separate development has not only needed to address but also redress its inheritance. They were trying to ensure that the pedagogy in Year R – this first year of schooling – should address the diverse realities of South Africa's children and the principles which underpin a participatory or enquiry democracy. Such a pedagogy would be based on a socio-cultural historical theoretical perspective closely related to the ideas of Vygotsky, which focus on *the nurturing of a reasonable person (both learner and teacher) in the context of a play-based Grade R (reception year)*' (Linington *et al.* 2011: 36). This **relational pedagogy** can be said to be the provision of contexts for learning where the learners are able to connect new learning to their own prior knowledge and cultural experiences, or what Jerome Bruner called each learner's 'cultural toolkit" (Bruner 1996). The implication is that each child's experience is accepted as valid and legitimate. This is very easy to understand in the context of South Africa's history where some – the majority of children – could not sit in the same classroom, swim in the same sea, read the same books as others, purely because of the colour of their skin. It also assumes the inclusion of the child's voice and the participation of the child as thinker, which may challenge the teachers to adopt different roles, which could be those of enquirer, guide, listener or democrat. Linington *et al.* claim that the socio-cultural approach is about play and imagination and collaborative learning; the learners – that is, the children together with the educators, become a community of enquiry, which, say the authors, leads to a pedagogy that emphasises reasoning, tolerance and inclusion. The language of the piece is sometimes difficult to unpick but in essence what they are saying is that, in the South African context, with the country's recent history, post-apartheid democratic citizenship requires not only that young children be communicative democrats but also that schools and preschools are not hierarchical or authoritarian, but rather places of reason. Burbules (1995) says that it is essential to see reasoning as a *situated embodied human practice* (which is a very complicated way of saying that making sense of the world is achieved through our bodies – through our perceptions, movements, emotions and actions), which is neither a universal nor a necessary mechanical application of logical rules, but should be

> sensitive to cultural difference and diversity; modest about its claims to universality; situated in human relations and moral reflection; grounded in more practical, social activities of speaking, listening and reflecting than in dispassioned logical deduction or a scientistic search for 'facts'.
>
> (Burbules 1995: 87–88)

The rights of children vis à vis the environment

In the *United Nations Convention on the Rights of the Child* (UNROC; Unicef 1989) Article 13, it states that the child should have the right to freedom of expression, which includes the freedom to seek and receive and give information and ideas of all kinds, regardless of frontiers and this may be orally or in writing or in print or through any other media. All children have the right to education and this includes the encouragement to develop and maintain respect for the environment. These and other rights illustrate the responsibilities of living in a free society and learning about respect for others and for the natural world. Essentially children should have the rights to participate and contribute their thoughts and ideas in any situation. To illustrate this we will examine a research study in a New Zealand city kindergarten which had a particular focus on the environment and is one of a small number of kindergartens participating in a New Zealand-wide *Enviroschools* programme established in the late 1990s. Mackey was a respected researcher in that setting and her initial aim was to identify how the young children and the adults set about exploring ideas and making decisions. The focus on rights only emerged after some observation of the interactions between children and children, and adults and children. Four themes or rights emerged. They were the right to know; the right to have your contribution heard and valued; the right to find a solution and the right to take action.

The right to know

At morning snack time this conversation was recorded.

> *Researcher: What bowl did you put the food in for the worms?*
> *Child 1: I think this one.*
> *Researcher: Oh, OK. And what sort of food do they like?*
> *Child 1: They eat bread, but not meat. Did you know worms are vegetarian?*
> (Mackey 2012: 478)

I love how this child is knowledgeable, communicative and offering her knowledge to the adult. And she certainly behaves as though she is aware that she is entitled to know things.

The right to have your contribution valued

A little boy (whom you met earlier in the book) expressed his concerns for baby penguins, thinking they might die of cold. He set about making a penguin saving device from pieces in a plastic construction kit.

> *Child: This machine can actually save the penguins.*
> *Teacher: Oh look.*
> *Child: The baby penguins.*
> *Teacher: Oh, I'd like to hear about that, Liam, Tell me how it saves the penguins.*
> *Child: You use it when it is very snowy. It can land on the sea and it can land on the ice. It's all right if one bit falls off because you can put it back together again.*
> (Mackey 2012: 479)

Another wonderful child able to identify a problem, seek and make a solution and explain it all to an adult.

The right to find a solution

Sadly there is no delightful anecdote to illustrate this but here is what a teacher said about how the staff in the kindergarten encourage children to share their ideas about solving a problem.

> *When the children come up with an idea, I think sometimes what we do really well is to carry on with it, to follow through quickly. I think it's important that if a child has an idea or we have an idea or something that's relevant at that time, we don't wait too long. Having the confidence to just go ahead and do the best that we can to see their needs is something I've only just learned to do – to give it a go.*
>
> (Mackey 2012: 480)

A reflective and honest teacher doing just what the children are doing, which is to find a solution.

The right to take action

This is possibly the most difficult for young children but once they observe more confident children they start to join in. And the more they do it the more confident they become. A little girl in the kindergarten who washed out her yoghurt pot told the teacher why she had done so and was praised. She did it again and is very likely to have the confidence to take action and celebrate doing so in the future.

The rule of all by all

Peter Moss (2007) writes that, for democratic politics and practice to come into the nursery, all those involved need to be engaged in four types of activity:

(1) They need to be able to *make decisions* about how the nursery should work – its purposes, practices and environment.
(2) They need to be able to *evaluate how well the nursery is working* – for example, how the children are engaged, how and what they are learning, how they are forming a culture and community.
(3) How they are *challenging the dominant discourse*. This is not easy to explain but, put more simply, this means being true to the values and principles of those who are trying to establish democracy in the nursery and willing to justify this.
(4) Moss calls this fourth feature being *open for change* or transformation.

For any system to be democratic those involved need to share some principles and ideas. For an early childhood setting to be truly democratic it requires that all those involved – the children, their parents or carers, the staff at all levels – are agreed on the following.

This is my list, based on that of Moss.

• A *recognition of and respect for diversity* so that that all children are welcomed in the setting and their languages and cultures reflected in practice. This must be shared by all so that children with special or particular needs are catered for and supported and they are truly integrated in all aspects of the setting.

- *A willingness to stand up and be heard and to defend ideas* that are possibly not those of the people who are in power. This may mean having the courage and the ability to challenge and defend ideas and practice.
- *A welcome for curiosity, uncertainty and subjectivity* so that adults and children can ask questions, query decisions, voice their opinions and needs and disagree with others.
- *A recognition of different perspectives and opinions and a range of paradigms* so that there is not only one way of doing things but choices. Children's voices are equal to those of adults.
- *Evidence of critical thinking by children and adults.* This means that everyone involved has the right to question or disagree with ideas, practice, theories, accepted wisdom and rules.
- *Documenting what children say and do* as a record of their thoughts and ideas, the ways in which these change and develop. This makes progress visible and opens possibilities of dialogue with and between different groups.

Moving on . . .

In this chapter we have looked at democracy and the consequences of asking very young children to make choices and decisions and to play the role of citizen by caring about what other children think and do and be prepared to not only give their opinion but also listen to the ideas of others. In the next chapter we look at the OMEP World Project. We turn our attention to sustainability.

Chapter 5

The OMEP World Project

Key words and concepts: research; formal, informal and non-formal education; single issues; patterns of production and consumerism; social, economic, political, cultural and generational aspects of sustainability; child-oriented perspective; learning; dialogue; right to express ideas, make decisions, change minds, join in, try, reject; community of practice; indigenous knowledge; poverty; 7Rs; sustainable development goals, lifelong learning.

During the last decade it became apparent that the damage we have done and continue to do to our planet was going to have to be tackled, and in order for this to happen significant changes in our values and behaviour and awareness are essential. Much of the burden will fall on the shoulders of our children and grandchildren and their children and grandchildren. UNESCO had declared the *United Nations Decade of Education for Sustainable Development* (ESD) to be 2005–2014 with its goal to involve and strengthen the roles of formal, informal and non-formal education – learning that takes place away from traditional schools or colleges – and integrate the values, principles and practices of sustainable development in all aspects of learning and education. ESD has the *roles of* (a) reorienting education in order to promote research and (b) discuss and disseminate findings so that sustainable development becomes a key theme at all levels. The *aims* are clearly to effect a change in human attitudes, behaviours, values, activities and principles. Important as they are we can no longer settle for talking about environmental education or dealing with single issues like reducing pollution. For a sustainable world we have to alter our patterns of production and consumption. We have to think more carefully about the impact of what we do in our everyday lives not only on the environment but on the people and creatures who live on this planet.

The World Organisation for Early Childhood Education (OMEP), which is a non-governmental, not-for-profit and international organisation concerned with all aspects of early childhood and care, is tasked with defending and promoting the rights of the child to education and care throughout the world and supports activities which will enable more young people gain access to high-quality care and education. We have already seen that early childhood education and care has been concerned with some aspects of sustainability for generations through an emphasis on using the outdoors, encouraging young children to care for small animals, focusing on domestic play and encouraging young children to care for one another and for their environment. Good early childhood education and care has also encouraged children to ask questions and invent worlds, which may be better than the ones they currently daily live in. This is an important point because we tend to link sustainability to the natural world, which makes sense, but the implications for people are enormous. Good education for sustainability will have to consider the social, economic, political, cultural and generational aspects as well. It was the awareness of this that made OMEP decide to carry out some research into what young children know and feel about the earth, about the environment, the responsibilities they and others have, who does what, what is good and what is harmful.

The theoretical underpinning of the project

Ingrid Engdahl (2015) wrote an account of the project, which I will quote from throughout this chapter. The organisers of the project decided to invite early childhood teachers/practitioners who had experience of children's attempts at making and sharing meaning to work with young children in order to find out what the children thought and felt and had experienced with regard to aspects of sustainability. The teachers involved would be the experienced adults trying to see the world through the eyes of the children. Such a child-oriented perspective is built on an interpretative psychological approach to early care combined with a child-oriented approach to early education, which is explained/presented in detail in Sommer et al. (2013). With a basis in the UN Convention on the Rights of the Child (UNICEF 1989), which has been ratified by 192 countries, a rationale is introduced that spells out and draws attention to the implications of giving young children a voice, having responsibilities, listening to them and trusting them as competent individuals.

In an attempt to get inside what is called a child-oriented perspective, adults would observe and listen to children with the intention of trying to see and hear and experience the world through their eyes or from their perspective. We know that children learn from the social world – certainly from the adults and from the children with whom they interact. They learn from watching what they do, hearing what they say, and taking note of what pleases them and what makes them sad or angry. They do this through looking, listening, using gesture and movement and language, experience and feelings. They are interpreting, reproducing and creating their own culture. As they make sense of the world they also make judgements about what is right and wrong, good and bad, useful and wasteful. In doing this they behave like little citizens.

In the project it was emphasised that the dialogues and communication between adult and child should be respectful and relate and conform to the conventions of where these take place and between whom. You will know that ways of being polite or acceptable will vary from place to place. It is likely that the ways in which adults and children communicate and share their thoughts in different cultures vary. It is important that the adults come to be able to refer to and understand all aspects of the lives of children including indigenous and traditional knowledge where appropriate. In short, the role of the adults was to recognise and respect children's rights to express their ideas, make decisions, change their minds, join in, comment on, suggest, try, reject and more.

An outline of the project

Two World Project coordinators were appointed, each a senior lecturer at a European university. A letter of invitation was sent to roughly 70 countries throughout the world together with instructions and formats so that the final results could be compared. There were to be four studies all with the aim of enhancing the awareness of ESD amongst OMEP members, young children and early childhood education staff. The project involved both action research and development projects. Action research can be research initiated to solve an immediate problem or it can also be a reflective process of progressive problem solving led by individuals working with others in teams or as part of a 'community of practice' to improve the way they address issues and solve problems. Developmental projects are more subject to requirements for early childhood education in their cities or countries. For example where there is a fixed curriculum in a country a developmental project would fit more easily than action research.

Study 1: Children's voices for sustainable development

In this study, children aged from 2 to 8 were shown a drawing of the earth and their comments, queries, suggestions and thoughts were given to the adults during informal interviews. The figures are astounding: 9,142 children took part in this in 385 settings in 35 countries. In the picture the children are looking at the earth, which is shown to be melting or dissolving. The children in the picture are shown cleaning the earth or trying to mend it in some way. The interview questions were: *Please look at this picture. Tell me about this picture. What is going on? Tell me more. What can you see in the picture?*

Follow-up questions included: *Why are they doing this? Anything more you want to tell me about the picture? Anything else that has to do with the things we have talked about?*

Study 2: Education for sustainable development in practice

The results from Study 1 were so interesting that the directors of the programmes decided to incorporate some of the issues addressed in the second study. Two questions were asked, as follows:

(1) *What do you think is NOT sustainable here in our centre/preschool/school?* and
(2) *How can we change this together?*

This was a much smaller study than Study 1 and I was interested to read that almost half of those responding in this study were from Russia. During the project there was some interest in developing and addressing topics nationally or locally. Seven words starting with the letters RE in English, French and Spanish and all linked to sustainability were offered up as possible discussion starting points.

 Can you identify which of the three fundamental aspects of sustainability each reflects? You will remember that the three pillars of ESD are the socio-cultural, the environmental and the economic.

(1) respect   the rights of the child
(2) reflect   on the cultural differences in the world
(3) rethink   people today value other things
(4) reuse   make more use of things
(5) reduce   we can do more with less
(6) recycle   someone else can use it again
(7) redistribute   resources can be used more equally

Respect, rethink and reflect relate clearly to the socio-cultural spectrum; reuse and reduce to the environmental aspects; and recycle and redistribute to the economic.

Study 3: Intergenerational dialogues about education for sustainable development

An interesting study considering how children learn from those older, younger and the same age with a focus on three themes – reducing plastic, growing food and making friends through play. In addition to the three dimensions mentioned above, this study included a focus on the political dimension of empowerment. The specific questions asked and follow-up activities were:

Question Activity

Question	Activity
How do we use plastic?	*Let's reduce the number of plastic bottles and bags in the setting or at home.*
Where does our food come from?	*Let's make a new garden in our neighbourhood to grow food.*
How do you play with other children and toys?	*Let's make new friends in another school or setting or neighbourhood. Let's make friends who are different from us in some way.*

Note: the last suggestion is mine and is not in the study.

Study 4: Equality for sustainability

The focus of this study is on the social and environmental, with a particular emphasis on the impact of poverty. When you talk to people about sustainability, poverty is often not mentioned and yet it is one of the most important factors. To broaden the scope of this study it extended its brief to other aspects of equity by considering those with special needs, gender issues, ethnicity, position of indigenous peoples and more.

In all four studies children of all ages were eager to talk and express their opinions and their concerns after viewing drawings or discussing the RE words. Not surprisingly, where the children chose topics that were meaningful to them they gave the most creative suggestions for future things to consider.

Listen to children's thinking

What is fascinating about the OMEP project is the way in which the young children involved reacted to being treated as having ideas worth sharing. The adults involved in the project commented on the fact that children think differently from adults and they think about different things. We have much to learn from them.

- Children in a Kamchatka kindergarten started a project called *Just a Usual Plastic Bottle* where they counted all types of goods in a supermarket that were sold in plastic bottles and turned their attention to the types of bottles they found in the streets. They presented the shopkeepers with the results and through this realised that it was possible to live without plastic bottles.

- In a Swedish study called *Building bridges over time and space* teachers and children in a nursery looked at toys and their history. Most of the toys in their nursery were made of recycled materials unlike the manufactured toys found in the shops. Thinking about the differences, children, parents, teachers and grandparents got together to discuss what they had found. They all agreed that children like to play with toys whatever they are made of but they also said that today's children base their play on what they see on the television and media; older people stated that they had based their play on characters and stories in books. In South Africa during the apartheid era children used found and natural materials to create not only toys but also musical instruments. They used wire, bits of metal, discarded tins, paper and card, coconut shells, bits of bark, pebbles and elastic bands. I have a human figure made out of discarded plastic bags, sitting on a push along bicycle made out of wire, which I still treasure although it is falling apart.
- *What's in your fridge* was a project in a nursery in a very poor community in Western Australia. The teacher started off the project by asking the children what they would find in their fridge. The children began to draw the interior of their fridges and the foods that might be in it. Then the teacher gave them two photographs to look at – one of a fridge full of food and the other of a fridge almost empty. The children had a great deal to say and talked about having a lot of stuff and having little; having enough money and not; what constitutes healthy and unhealthy foods. Rather than delivering a talk about poverty, the teacher sensitively let the children arrive at their own ideas just through looking and listening to others. It is fascinating that the Aboriginal children in that study were the only ones to come up with ideas of where to find things that remain edible without having a fridge to store them in. A model of Indigenous knowledge!
- In the *Friendly hearts* project in Slovakia the children decided to have a toy day and to take a toy of theirs to the retirement home where the old people both talked about the toys they had had and also tried out the newer ones. Having a shared focus of attention led to a real exchange of ideas.
- When some young children were asked if they had heard of sustainable development and knew what it meant they answered like this:

  - A child in Brazil said '*Ensuring everyone a better future.*'
  - A child from Cameroon said '*It is to maintain the earth.*'
  - A Japanese child added '*It means being generous to the earth.*'
  - A child from Ireland said '*I think it might mean, like, to save the world for later.*'
  - And a Turkish child summed it all up by saying '*So that the earth is not to die and humans would need to live on another planet.*'

 ## What did you learn from the OMEP World Project?

I guess that what you learned will depend on what you already know. I had my ideas about young children being citizens, meaning makers, communicative, social, political, questioning beings confirmed. And I also had my ideas about how important it is in early education and care to listen to children, pay attention and take seriously what they say and do. And always ask yourself if you need a curriculum handed to you or if you can go from what the children are interested in.

The Sustainable Development Goals

It is important to know that in 2015 the United Nations (UN) developed a series of Sustainable Development Goals (SDGs), which, they said, should be achieved within 15 years. There were 17 goals in all and Goal 4 is the one that is most relevant to us here. It reads: *'Ensure inclusive and quality education for all and promote lifelong learning.'* An indicator for this (Goal 4.2) turns the spotlight on early years, stating that *'By 2030 ensure that all girls and boys have access to quality early childhood development, care and pre-primary education so that they are ready for primary education.'*

 Select the words in that last paragraph that you find most relevant to educating young children for sustainability.

I chose *inclusive*, *quality* and *lifelong learning* because they are inclusive in terms of gender and they address the issue of good learning, which is sustained through life. I do, however, have some difficulty with the concept of 'quality' in terms of how it is assessed or evaluated. I also feel a little uncomfortable with the concept of 'good' early childhood education being about preparing children for primary school.

Moving on . . .

In this chapter we returned to the focus on sustainability and learned about the OMEP World Project. In the next chapter we examine which pedagogy is most suited to educating young children for sustainability.

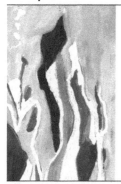

Chapter 6

A pedagogy for sustainability?

Key words and concepts: enabling; sustained learning; artist in residence; pedagogy of expression; pedagogy-in-participation; care-full pedagogy; ethics of care; shared responsibility; emotional intensity; hope of change through transformation.

Ingrid Pramling Samuelsson, whose work you have already encountered in this book, collaborated with Eunhye Park in writing a paper with the intriguing title of 'How to Educate Children for Sustainable Learning and for a Sustainable World' (2017). If we think about it, enabling and encouraging young children to *want* to keep on learning is essential and in doing it you will have the total support of parents, teachers, carers and others. There is evidence that many young children in this country are turned off formal education for a variety of reasons. Perhaps they are being taught things that are not relevant or interesting to them. Perhaps they feel judged and begin to fail because there are tests and exams. There is often a focus on what children don't know and cannot yet do rather than on what they can do and what they are interested in. Young children need to be supported when they question or seek help. They need to have opportunities to work with others in order to share ideas and have pleasure in their learning. Learning should be social and closely linked to culture. The authors tell us that '*Values related to sustainability promote a certain type of pedagogy in which the child should be allowed to take initiatives, think and reflect*' (2017: 1).

 What pedagogy or philosophy of learning do you think is most likely to promote a love of learning?

This is a very difficult and contentious question but what the authors of this paper say is that, in order to promote a pedagogy for sustainability, there must be the following values:

- Both staff and parents view children as competent and receptive.
- Children are invited, encouraged and supported in following their own passions and interests.
- All staff are appropriately trained to know how to follow children's initiatives and listen attentively.
- Parents or carers are regarded as partners in the child's learning not only at home but also in the early years setting.
- All staff and parents are aware of what is relevant for young children learning about sustainability.

Where young children are treated as serious thinkers we have to accept that much of what they think about is the world they inhabit and the people and animals and insects and plants they share it with. Children notice what is happening around them and hear people talking about events large and small. What they see and hear might make them happy or sad, frightened or excited, curious or anxious. The best early childhood provision takes account of children's feelings and recognises the significance of the children being able to express their feelings in some way. Pedagogy may be defined simply as the method or art and science of teaching. A fuller definition suggests that it means the set of instructional techniques and strategies which enable learning to take place and provide opportunities for the acquisition of knowledge, skills, attitudes and dispositions within a particular social and material context. This second definition, often used in connection to early learning, pays attention to the social nature of both learning and teaching but does not mention emotion. Some claim that pedagogy refers to both the interactive process between teacher and learner and to the learning environment (Siraj-Blatchford *et al.* 2002). What this means is that the provision includes things that may interest children and invite them to ask questions or employs adults who are not necessarily teachers but do some visible work in a place that is accessible to the children. The prime example comes again from Reggio Emilia. There is an artist (or *atelierista/o* in residence) based in a studio to which all children have easy and ongoing access. Malaguzzi insisted that there should be one in every nursery and he called the studio a '*subversive eruption*', and Gandini (2005: 7) said that the

> role of the atelier, integrated and combined within the general framework of learning and teaching strategies, was conceptualised as a retort to the marginal and subsidiary role commonly assigned to expressive education. It was also intended as a reaction against the concepts of education of young children based mainly on words and simple-minded rituals.

This is a piece that is worth re-reading because there is so little that focuses on the deep significance for all children to be able to express their feelings. Education should be as much about feelings as it is about cognition.

A pedagogy of expression

Certainly the best known and most influential examples of a pedagogy of expression are to be found in the provision in Reggio Emilia and also in other Italian regions. And there are other places where there is a focus on offering opportunities for the children to express their feelings through dancing and singing, making things, drawing, painting, telling stories and imaginative play. It is important to consider how this pedagogy matches the concept of sustainability. The worlds of young children are complex and globalisation has added to the complexity but wherever children live – in towns or cities, farms or townships, refugee camps or hostels, in tents or houses or apartment blocks or slums, by the sea, in the mountains or the desert – they are affected by what happens around them and also by things they see on the television or on screens that they can view. Like the children talking about the Zeebrugge disaster, they see and hear things that may delight them but may also distress them.

 Go into a nursery setting or children's library or bookshop and look at the picture books then work out the percentage that you see that address aspects of sustainability.

Picture books, narrative, whose stories are these?

The abundance of picture and story books for young children in the developed world is extraordinary. I am not talking about primers or worthy books teaching children to count or sound out words or discover that Peter is here but Jane is not. I am thinking of children's literature, which is an extraordinary resource. I have never met a young child who does not love to be read to, look at the pictures and escape into other worlds. Quality children's literature deals with real issues set in real or imagined or created worlds and is all about living creatures or created creatures and about where and how they live, what problems they encounter, their adventures, their fears, their struggles and their feelings. Children's literature leads children into knowing more about their world and becoming able to construct worlds of their own. Many traditional tales deal with real issues like life and death, just and unjust, rich and poor, old and young, power and weakness. Postmodern literature takes from these tales and subverts them in some way. Brian Simons, a teacher I knew well, asked his class of 7 year olds if they might like to draw up a petition for the rights of the poor troll whose life was being ruined by the greed of the *Three Billy Goats Gruff*. The children became quickly involved in heated discussion about who was right and who was wrong. Fairness is an issue relevant to them in everyday life and in terms of sustainability.

Picture books allow very young children to decide for themselves what is happening and create their own narrative. Suzy Lee made a beautiful wordless book called *Wave*. Liliana, aged 4, looked at the book, turning the pages and making up her own monologue, which went like this:

> *'No words. No words. Is it a book? It is a book. She is with her mum on the beach and there's birds. And the sea is blue and wavy. She looks a little scared. I went to the beach. I found shells. Look, here's shells. The wave dropped the shells for her. Now she's going home with her mum and she's waving goodbye.'*

> (Smidt 2012: 49)

This picture book contained images that enabled this young child to not only make sense of what was happening but also to make links with her own experience. She was making sense of the whole book, paying attention to how she thought the little girl was feeling and invented a very personal reason for the waves to be on the beach. Compare Liliana's response with that of Rifat, a 7-year-old refugee who looked at the same book. His teacher noted that he looked at the book with intent concentration and went back to pore over the book every day over a week. Then, one day, he brought the book to the teacher and said '*Sea . . . boat. Me in boat come London*'. How different a personal response from that of Liliana.

Cutting out and sticking; recognising what you have achieved

Some expressive activities are more recognised as being 'useful' than others, as Gunther Kress noted. Children drawing and building and talking are doing things that are regarded as being 'good' whereas cutting and sticking may be labelled as 'just play' and disregarded. Kress was in search of the paths to literacy: I am interested here in the relation of these activities to expressing feelings. Kress offers us the example of a 4-year-old girl sitting and kneeling on chairs with her two friends around the kitchen table. They were cutting shapes out of large sheets of paper. Holding up her creation the little girl shrieked '*My Gawd, I made it like Australia!*' (1997: 34). Kress has no explanation of her link, if any, to Australia. What he focuses on is that the child is aware of both agency and ownership, both essential to developing self-esteem. He tells us that

> *cutting out may offer the child one means of bridging a gap between two kinds of imaginative worlds, one in which the child 'enters the page' so to speak, and imaginatively enters into the life of objects in or on the page; and another in which represented objects come off the page and are brought into the world of physical objects here and now, which are then reanimated in the imaginative effort of the child. There is a then a continuum for the child between things on the page – one kind of distanced intangible reality; and things here and now, another kind of reality, not distanced but tangible. The two kinds of realism are linked through the actions of the child.*
>
> (Kress 1997: 27)

I find it utterly impossible to analyse how and why the child thought she had made a map of Australia!

 But did you think her reaction to what she thought she had achieved was joyous? Why?

In much of early childhood provision in parts of Italy like Reggio Emilia, Pistoia and Sant'Ilario d'Enza, children are recognised as competent citizens and everything that happens in the provision is based around the expressed interests of the children. The underpinning philosophy is that if children are interested in something they will have some emotional attachment to it. There is no set curriculum and the staff in all the settings work as a team, and although their roles and training differ they come together for regular in-service training.

Walking and talking, drawing and painting, having your work celebrated

To illustrate this I want to share with you some of the things said by children and recorded by their teachers and carers in the Fiastri and Rodari Municipal Preschools in Sant'Ilario d'Enza in Italy. The children (all aged under 7) had been exploring ideas about time and it was then that the word 'future' was used. The children wanted to talk about what they understood about the future and then began to think what things might be like in the future. Out of that a project emerged and so astounding were the children's ideas and images that a book was produced by their colleagues in Reggio Emilia. The result is the book called *The Future Is a Lovely Day*.

The future is an abstract concept; no young children can know what it means unless they have heard adults talking about it or encountered it on television or in the cinema or in picture books.

 Read some of the comments below made by the children to get some appreciation of their understanding or imagining of sustainability. It is never

mentioned, but the children, working on what they already know, are attempting to predict in startling ways.

Some small examples to start with:

*   '*In the future there will be lots of water and less land, there'll be lots of sea,*' said Matteo.
*   '*We'll never be all equal, that's a dream, it can't happen,*' said Elena.
*   '*A million years from now it'll be dirty everywhere, people'll have to wear anti-stink masks,*' said Mariam.

As the project continued, the children expanded their original thoughts and dictated these to the staff who wrote them out for them.

*   Claudio said: '*To go on living on the land – and there won't be much – we'll have to build the houses on a kind of table laid on an iron pipe that's planted in the ground. I'd make it with a piston that makes it go up and down. Usually they are kept high so there's more room on the ground. I'd put wheels on the houses too so you can move about more quickly from one place to another.*'
*   Clarissa (pointing to her drawing) said: '*This pony of the future will have to become lighter so it can fly and the tube it's got in its tummy will open and then it'll fly with its wings. On its face there's a ball that's already there when it's born and it's full of air. You know – the babies come through the tube when they're born . . . . The fish won't be able to stay in the polluted sea. They'll have wings for flying.*'
*   Davide said: '*In the future it'll rain more and more and there'll be more trees. There'll be more fruit on trees 'cause there'll be more of us. There will be lots of us! So there'll have to be lots more fruit otherwise it won't be enough. The trees will have to be terribly tall so there will be more fruit and more birds. There'll be triangular-shaped pine trees that won't bear fruit – they'll just be for the birds' homes. Then there'll be fruit trees that'll make so much fruit that there won't be any room for birds' nests. They'll be separate so the birds won't eat all the fruit. They'll have to have lots of enormous roots to keep them firm on the ground.*'

A house that goes up and down with a piston! Fish with wings. Terribly tall trees with so much fruit on them leaving no room for birds' nests – the amazing ideas of very young children. The book was published in 2001 so these children will probably have their own children by now. I wonder what *their* ideas about the future will be like.

Note: I have a much loved copy of the book, which is lavishly illustrated by the children: *Il futuro e una bella giornata* (*The Future Is a Lovely Day*). Reggio Children, 2001/2003.

A care-full pedagogy

Let's look at another kind of pedagogy, this time based on a paper entitled 'Maternal thinking and beyond: towards a care-full pedagogy for early childhood' by Paulette Luff and Mallika Kanyal (2015). The title of this piece is intriguing because of the way in which the word 'careful' is made to mean not cautious but full of care.

In early childhood education provision there has been, and still is, in some places a dual system: one for education and one for care. In general those working in the care settings have qualifications in care and those in the education settings have qualifications in education. Anyone who has worked in a nursery class or school knows how important it is to deal with not only the intellectual part of learning but also the emotional. To educate children without care seems to me to be impossible. Yet, in the UK at least, while training programmes for teaching assistants and nursery nurses contain reference to care, many training programmes for teachers contain very little. But there is increasing awareness of the benefits for young children of being in settings where they are offered both care and education, and this is rapidly developing globally.

The ethics of care

Much has been written about the ethics of care and much of it is rather confusing. The clearest account I have come across is that of Peter Moss in his musings on a conference he had attended in Stockholm in 2001. He points out that the word 'care' can mean different things according to the context in which it is used. The word 'care' in relation to what is on offer for working parents does not mean the same as caring for or caring about someone or something. Moss chooses to think of care as an ethic. Many feminist thinkers and philosophers were interested in the ethics of care and one of these women, Joan Tronto, said that an ethics of care is about *'a practice rather than a set of rules and principles. . . . It involves particular acts of caring and a "general habit of mind"'* (1993: 127). In her view, care is a political and a moral concept through which we can make judgements about aspects of the public world – like early childhood education and care. Importantly, care helps us to reexamine humans as being interdependent beings.

 What do you think interdependent means and what is its relevance?

Interdependent means depending on one another. It makes clear that in any social exchange there are two or more people, each with ideas, values, lives, a history and a future. Moss goes on to say that care itself has four elements: caring about, taking care of, care giving and care receiving. An ethic of care has a further four elements: responsibility, competence, integrity and responsiveness. As I said earlier, this is all rather many layered but in essence much of this is common sense when you think about human relationships. What we learn from this is that in any exchange between a child and adult the adult must see the child and put the needs or feelings of the child first or, as Emmanuel Levy (Levinas) put it, 'I am responsible for the other immediately when he looks at me without me *taking* responsibility for him' (1996: 78).

In any early childhood setting you will see adults caring for the children. They wipe away tears, cut a bruised knee, hold on to the hand of a child frightened of something, intervene in disputes and reassure newcomers. But more significantly they spend much of their time establishing and renewing relationships with the children. It is still a field where woman are in the majority, which may account for it to be still undervalued and its practitioners seen as 'just nursery teachers'. The care-full pedagogy of Luff and Kanyal requires what the authors call *maternal intellectual considerations*. In essence what they are saying is that practitioners should seek to establish maternal-like relationships with young children. These might include the daily tasks of setting up the room and resources and making careful observations – so watching, listening and interacting with small children just as a mother might do. More than that, the authors suggest that attentive relationships between carer and cared-for might extend to child–child, child–practitioner, child–content, practitioner–practitioner and so on. So the adults care for the children and the children care for one another and the children care about the adults and about the things they are doing and the adults care about one another.

Case Study 6: The life of chickens

Ingrid Engdahl and Eva Ärlemalm-Hagsér (2008) examined one project that came about through some questions asked by a group of 5–6-year-olds in Långvik's preschool, which is outside Stockholm. The children began to ask questions related to life and the quality of life. This was no simple project, as the questions suggest. Children in this nursery are accustomed to asking questions when they notice something that interests or concerns them. In asking questions and looking for answer they are using what Malaguzzi called the 'hundred languages'. In this case the children developed an interest in eggs and chickens. Their questions included 'Why do some eggs have chickens inside and some don't?' and 'Which animals are born from eggs?' These seem to me to be pretty complex questions. The children visited a farm and made their own hens out of paper and went on to build cages and 'houses' for them. They talked about what it must feel like to be a hen and wondered if being human was better or worse. They developed a concern that some chickens had free movement and some lived in cages. In this way it seems they were exploring existential and ethical aspects of being a hen. Through both their questions and their actions they were querying and considering our shared responsibility as humans for nature. Finally, they asked the preschool's cook what eggs she used and were appalled by the answer – eggs from hens in cages. We have already established that these young children are thinkers and have already developed a sense of what is just and what is unjust.

 Can you guess what path the children decided to follow?

They decided to follow a political process involving the municipal office, the directors of education and finance and the local egg producers. They were acting as citizens operating democratically like some of the children you encountered earlier in this book. You will, perhaps, not be surprised that their protests were successful – the rules were changed and all preschools in this municipality were allowed to buy eggs from ecologically certified farms. All teachers, the children's families and relatives also switched to eggs from hens with the best living conditions!

I love this little example of young children demonstrating ethical care. The authors tell us that this theme 'covered the three ESD components – ecological, social and economic – and it was initiated and conducted by the children, thus performed in a democratic and empowering way, ensuring participation and influence for all learners, which is also a fundamental aspect of ESD' (Engdahl & Ärlemalm-Hagsér 2008: 118).

And what about Pedagogy-in-Participation?

Our focus so far has largely been on children between the ages of 3 and 7. Let us now consider what adults working with children under 3 can do to extend and support their learning. This comes from an article by Julia Oliveira-Formosinho and Sara Barros Araújo (2011) called 'Early education for diversity: Starting from birth' and clearly influenced by the work of Colwyn Trevarthen and Rosemary Roberts, both of whom focus very clearly on the competent, communicative, problem-solving meaning-making infant or young child. Their thesis is that every practitioner must approach the work with young children **with respect for their capabilities** and consider the **emotional intensity of each interaction**, create situations and an environment which **fosters the agency of the child** and the building and respecting of **companionable relationships with and between the children**. It is just those values held by practitioners that will make them excellent educators for educating the younger children for a sustainable planet.

You will appreciate just how focused these authors are on key themes related to sustainability: (a) respect for children as questioning meaning makers; (b) on the social and emotional aspects of learning; and (c) on the agency of the child. Their important paper starts by deploring the relative lack of research into very young children's competence and particularly into young children's feelings and responses to diversity. This depends largely on where in the world the children are but there is evidence that very young children notice differences in skin colour, hair structure and shapes of nose and eyes, and can display positive or negative attitudes to people who look different from them. Glenda MacNaughton argued that children at the age of 3 could not only be certain of their gender and identity but also knew what playthings and clothing were assumed to be appropriate for them. She wrote this nearly 30 years ago and there is hope that this has changed. The paper we are concerned with here was written only 7 years ago and is thinking about what teachers and carers need to think about and offer in order to educate children to view diversity with respect.

 This is an important subject, so consider what you think the most important issues students or practising teachers need to learn and/or implement in their practice.

My suggestions are:

- They need to think carefully about what style of teaching or pedagogy would facilitate an education for diversity.
- They would need to consider how to empower themselves and those they work with to genuinely respect diversity and difference and be open to change.
- They might have to think very carefully about how to assess the success or not of the changes they make.
- They need to think about the importance of equality and democracy, the rights of everyone, (adults and children), and become adept at empowering the children through the respect shown to them.

The solution?

Julia Oliveira-Formosinho and Sara Barros Araújo (2011) say that the solution is in two parts. First there is the role of pedagogy, and they emphasise the importance of children learning in the real world as part of the real world and about the real world. In this way they have the chance to make decisions, select what to make or do, how to do it and with whom, where and when and how. You will recognise the part played by democracy and also see the similarities with the provision in Reggio Emilia. Attention needs to be paid to the resources on offer so it is clear that there is not only one way of being in the world so the ethnicity and language and gender and cultures of the children find their way into the world of the nursery.

Adults need to be empathetic observers and documenters of what children say and do, make and enjoy, fear and avoid.

To understand the second part you need to become familiar with the Portuguese word *conscientizacao* used very often by the wonderful Brazilian educationalist Paolo Freire, which, loosely translated, means something like the hope of change through transformation. In short the goal is a pedagogy of listening and answering. In the words of Oliveira-Formosinho and Barros Araújo,

> *Pedagogy-in-Partnership aims at the creation of educational centres as democratic spaces, characterised by the respect for all individuals and groups involved in educational processes, by the promotion of intercultural dialogues, by collaboration in learning journeys, by intentional educational experiences that centrally contribute for the development of plural identities and multiple relations, and in which is interwoven learning about the self, the others, about relations, interactions, connections and ties, having permanently in mind the respect for human rights.*

(2011: 234)

Lenira Haddad, also a Brazilian educationalist, discusses the

> *specific dignity of early childhood education which she sees as an essential part of achieving a sustainable society. What she means is that as early childhood education becomes an important system in its own right with its own identity, it must become able to open up dialogue between the needs of civil society and the resources available for children and their families. Discussion needs to include the issues around gender roles, the balance between family and working life, the upbringing of children who spend some time beyond the traditional boundaries of family life and the everyday and intense relationships that characterise the volatile emotional lives of young children. The issue is that old paradigms need to be challenged if this special dignity is to be achieved. I wonder if you feel we need a similar debate in this country.*

(Smidt 2014: 61)

Developmental pedagogy

In their article 'The Playing Learning Child: Towards a Pedagogy of Early Childhood', Pramling Samuelson and Asplund Carlsson offer an example of what they term developmental pedagogy, which is what the teacher does to extend the child's experience.

 Read through this delightful description of Hjalmar aged 16 months as he works or plays in the kitchen. Is he working or playing and does it matter what we call it?

Case Study 7: Hjalmar in control

Hjalmar opens a large drawer in the kitchen, exploring all the objects that are there, and turns all the knobs on the oven. He then takes out a lot of kitchen tools. All the plastic bowls are sorted according to size. He experiments, changes his mind a few times. He then begins to put back all the kitchen tools and bowls into the drawer. Suddenly he bends down and lifts up a plastic bowl with both hands, pretending that it is heavy and groaning 'Oh, oh!' He does this twice. And finally he stops a little bit from the drawer, takes aim with the last object and throws it into the drawer.

(Samuelsson & Carlsson 2008: 624)

This is a wonderful illustrative example of how unpredictable and sometimes difficult to interpret the behaviour of young children can be. It is tempting to think that Hjalmar might just be messing around but my instincts tell me that he is doing something serious in order to understand the world around him. No one told him what to do or indeed interacted with him. He explored objects, making judgements about size and type. In doing this he was beginning to understand some mathematical concepts – big, small, heavy, light, square, like a ball or flat like a book? He pretended that the bowl he picked up was heavy, so he groaned just as he has seen and heard other people do. He was repeating something he has seen and played out his own versions. And he demonstrated his physical prowess by tossing the last piece into the drawer. Whether we label this as play or work does not matter. What does matter is that he is learning.

 What would you have said to Hjalmar had you been there with him?

One of the most powerful tools you have is your ability to notice what the child knows and can do, take it seriously and give the child praise which is focused on his or her achievement. How the adult responds to the child is very significant and something that can affect the child's confidence, self-image and willingness to do things in front of 'an audience'. I am reminded of what happened to me in a nursery class many years ago. A new child, Homa, had started that morning and I asked Jane, an old hand at being a nursery child, to take her to do a painting. When the girls had both finished, Homa took her painting off the easel and set off with it. Jane stopped her to ask, 'What are you doing?' Homa replied, 'Going to show the teacher.' 'No!' insisted Jane. 'She'll only tell you it's beautiful.'

 This seemingly trite example is actually a very serious thing to think about. How did that teacher respond to children's learning and what effect did that have on the children?

Giving empty praise – saying something is lovely, or 'very good', for example, is of no use to the learner. First of all it does not tell the child what it is that was good or lovely. Second, it doesn't help the child know how to do it differently or better next time.

 Try reading the feedback others might have given Hjalmar and evaluate them in terms of how they help the little learner as he moves on.

Farah said: 'Wow you have been busy!'

Marcus said: 'I liked the way you sorted all those plastic bowls. You put each one top of a bigger one, so you were sorting them by size. Could you sort them another way do you think?'

Archana said: 'I think you like turning on knobs, throwing things and lifting heavy weights.'

Livia said: 'Oh, Hjalmar – don't do that. It is dangerous!'

I liked how Marcus was able to focus on something he thought that Hjalmar had achieved and then offered him a suggestion of what he might do next time. What he did was give detailed and focused praise, which helped the child take the next step.

Case Study 8: Who owns this?

In the same paper, Pramling Samuelsson and Asplund Carlsson described a project that a teacher started in a nursery class and what happened after that. The child in question was 5 years old and in a preschool in Sweden. One morning in the classroom she said that toadstools are poisonous and this led to the the the children, together with the teacher, starting a project on mushrooms. As far as we know this was the expressed interest of only one child. The teacher had, in her mind, a possible learning outcome of the project, which was to encourage the children to discuss and develop symbols to pass on messages. The teacher then asked the little girl how she could let the other children know that the mushroom was poisonous and the child replied by saying, 'Write a note.' The response of the teacher was to ask 'Can young children read?'

Now a project on symbols could be interesting, relevant and appropriate at that stage when children are beginning to encounter and decode symbols: the numerals, for example, or the symbol for the London underground, and many more. The child here reacted very appropriately by drawing a mushroom and putting a cross through it. The child and teacher then talked for a while about mushrooms with the knowledgeable child drawing on her own experience of eating delicious and non-poisonous ones. At this level the child and teacher were exchanging ideas, perhaps allowing the child to start to understand that other people may have a different perspective from one's own. Samuelsson calls this developmental pedagogy where one of the roles of the teacher is to direct the attention of the learner towards the adult's learning goal.

 I wonder what you think about this.

Personally I am very wary of allowing the learning goals in the teacher's head to dictate what takes place. Where there is a prescribed curriculum which defines what the children should be learning, this is a common way of teaching. I think I might, instead, have asked the child if she could work with some other children in designing a symbol for some other situation. Teachers do, of course, have to take things forwards but they can do it by listening carefully and watching so that they get some insight into what the child or children are interested in. I wondered if the little girl who knew so much about mushrooms might have been more interested in finding out about them rather than conveying a message about a danger.

Now a vexed question. I wonder what you think about having to follow a curriculum. Do you think those working with young children need a curriculum or should the curriculum arise from the interests of the children?

For me this is the single most significant question to ask. If we are serious about early childhood education for sustainability we cannot operate with a curriculum set by people who do not know and value the children. The model of pedagogy that impresses me most remains that of Reggio Emilia and the other places where there are listening and reflective practitioners, who largely follow children's interests, support and extend them and document what they see and hear. The children are engaged in democratic meaning making and the staff in listening, resourcing, engaging and documenting this.

The beat of life in Reggio Emilia

Vea Vecchi wrote a short paragraph called 'Small gestures of solidarity' and I ask you to read it here and ask yourself what it tells you about young thinkers.

> On a sunny February day, Alice (4 years old) discovered some prematurely flowering violets like unexpected treasure close to a low wall. The following day in place of the sunny weather, a cold wind was blowing insistently and Alice, remembering the violets, went outside to build a makeshift shelter for them from dry leaves. Again, a little boy (2 years old) in a nido (nursery) found and gathered a rose from the ground as he was walking. He placed it on top of a low wall saying that it was 'going to sleep' and continued on his walk.
>
> (2010: 116)

It is evident that these very young children are demonstrating an awareness of how to protect and save living things. Vecchi poetically described the actions of children in regard to living things as having '*a beat of life which, if respected and opportunely supported, I am certain would help to construct knowledge that is not only more ethical and more based on solidarity but capable of a broader world vision*' (2010: 116).

Moving on . . .

In this chapter we made the link between sustainability and education by examining some of the pedagogies that are thought to be most successful for helping young children learn about all aspects that need to be considered for a sustainable world. In the next chapter we look at the vexed question of having early childhood care or early childhood education or early childhood care and education.

Chapter 7

The case for caring and learning together

Key words and concepts: care vs education; integrated provision; parents and professionals as partners; qualifications; pay and conditions; schoolification; universal access; ecological model.

We have already noted that in almost every country early childhood care and education (ECCE) have been and sometimes are still split between the two traditions, care and education. Care was initially developed as a concern for the welfare of children of working-class parents, who needed a safe place whilst their parents were at work earning a living. Education was developed as a service largely for the children of middle-class parents, wanting their children to have a good start in life by being engaged in what were seen to be educational activities carefully designed to meet the needs (if not, necessarily, the interests) of preschool age children. In this chapter we address whether this division of care vs education meets the needs of children and their families and if not what are the benefits of integrating or combining learning and care. The concerns are: (a) where the emphasis is primarily on education (as in a nursery school or nursery class in a school) care may not be seen as important yet we all know that that care is essential wherever young children are concerned; and (b) where the emphasis is on care alone (as in a childcare centre) the message might be that learning is not important yet we all know that children are learning wherever they are. Bringing care and education together seems an obvious solution but, as always, change is difficult and money is always an issue. Worldwide it is evident that governments have traditionally been more willing to fund education rather than care. In some countries care is still seen as the poor and rather distant relative of education.

In 2001 OECD and UNESCO reviewed the research done on the development and implementation of services for young children which were not split but coordinated and integrated. In such models it was believed that it should be possible that, by bringing care and education together, care and education would become the responsibility of society rather than primarily of the family. Where children are in such integrated provision the children of the rich and the poor, the fortunate and less fortunate, the haves and have nots, meet one another and socialise with one another. Differences are recognised and celebrated.

A South African saga

Soon after apartheid ended I went back to live and work in South Africa. I found the most interesting and challenging job and remained there for three years. I worked for an NGO trying to establish what the stakeholders in early childhood care and education throughout the country considered to be the basic 'norms and standards' for early childhood provision. After decades of apartheid or separate development, early childhood provision went from the most well resourced to having no resources and operating in a garage or under a tree or in an abandoned container. The new government was seeking to discover how to provide equity and opportunity for future generations. We were considering what the essentials things that all those working with young children needed to know and be able to do. I worked with a small team of young South Africans, all of whom spoke all 11 official languages whilst I struggled away with English and Afrikaans. The project was led by the new minister for education. We devised a set of criteria and then took these to huge workshops made up of stakeholders including teachers, childcare workers, university lecturers, local government staff, parents, funders and sometimes children themselves. We travelled throughout the country to have these norms and standards agreed or not. In the early post-apartheid years anyone could offer childcare anywhere – under a tree, in a garage, in a container or a church hall and with no running water, or no equipment or training. In response to the random and precarious existing provision we had no option but to consider issues of physical safety as primary, plus quality of education, health and community values and needs. For me our initial planning meetings were life changing. I had regarded myself as something of an 'expert'. I had, after all written books on the work of Vygotsky and Bruner but it soon became clear that whilst I fitted nicely into one box – education – the South African other members of the team knew far more about care. And care in South Africa meant survival. I had to learn the lesson that it makes no sense to separate education and care.

 Integrated settings are thought of as bringing together care and education on one site and working as a unit. Whose voices are missing, do you think?

The missing voices are, in my opinion, those of the parents of the children. They are, after all, essential key players in any decisions about young children.

The norms and standards we developed became law but were not enough to address the huge issue of how to reframe early childhood education and care so that equity and quality were addressed.

To redress this we are going to look at a research project in the Netherlands, described by Fuusje de Graaff and Anke van Keulen in an excellent paper published by the Bernard van Leer Foundation in 2008, and called 'Making the road as we go: Parents and professionals as partners managing diversity in early childhood education'. To contextualise the programme, here is some information from the book to help you understand the system of early childhood care and education in the Netherlands.

Early childhood care and education in the Netherlands

Childcare is the term used for all provision in the Netherlands for children aged up to 5 years and is provided by childcare centres, registered child minders, playschools and other preschool settings. Childcare has grown rapidly in the last 15 years, later than in many other European countries and is attributed to the increasing participation of Dutch women in the labour market. Approximately 20% of Dutch children aged

0–4 years now make use of childcare centres while about 60% of all 2- to 3-year-olds attend a playschool. The number of places has increased partly because of government efforts to offer early educational programmes for children who have an insufficient command of the Dutch language. These programmes prepare 3-year-olds (and their mothers) for the children's introduction into primary education at age 4, and particularly emphasise language skills.

Childcare is not funded by the government in the Netherlands, but is provided by businesses that operate in the free market and are subject to the Childcare Act, 2005. This act regulates the cost and quality of the childcare provided. Parents who are working or studying receive a government grant towards the cost of childcare with the level of these grants dependent on their incomes. In addition, some employers subsidise the costs of childcare.

Educators in the settings are required to have a professional qualification – a 4-year tertiary non-university qualification for managers and a 2- to 3 year secondary vocational education qualification for other staff. Childcare providers are supervised by municipal health services and must take into account municipal policy on special target groups, young people and children with special educational needs. The Childcare Act also lays down that parents have a formal right to advisory powers and can help determine childcare organisations' policies. It also stipulates that every childcare location has to have a parents' committee.

'Making the road as we go'

The parents involved were determined that the booklet was published for a number of reasons as follows:

- *to draw attention to recognising the significance of parents being involved in a research project based in childcare centres with the brief of looking at integrating diversity in how the centres are run;*
- *to set the research in the context of the wider project;*
- *to link the work of the project and the researchers to the wider field through a brief overview of the literature on parental involvement in childcare in the Netherlands;*
- *to consider how the awareness of diversity in parental participation can be quantified;*
- *to demonstrate that there are no standard formulas for establishing pedagogic partnerships with parents in childcare;*
- *to discuss the relationships between parents and professionals in childcare in terms of emotions and issues of concern;*
- *to identify what staff and parents talk about when they interact;*
- *to identify key issues in relation to the power relations between parents and educators; and*
- *to consider the implications for developing policies within childcare organisations for extending partnerships with parents (2008: V).*

This is interesting but perhaps you are questioning how this relates to sustainability, so let me remind you that what is vital if we are to save the planet is that we learn to listen and talk to, work with, respect and engage with as many people in our lives as possible. To do this we have to unlearn some behaviours and learn new ways of being citizens, parents, carers, teachers or just human.

One of the most significant acts of the Parents and Diversity project was that it attempted to quantify parental participation (how many parents were involved) and examined diversity in terms of the four concepts below:

(1) *living together*, which means sharing information;
(2) *working together*, which means deciding who does what, who makes the decisions, who follows;
(3) *thinking together*, which means talking together about ideas and concepts and actions and concerns.
(4) *taking decisions together*, meaning negotiating and agreeing.

You will recognise that teachers and staff are in very different positions in any setting. The teachers/carers know about and are responsible for the children at the setting but the parents know and care about their own children. The teachers/carers know about early childhood and care and the parents know about life away from the setting. There is a difference in the levels of power the two groups have.

 Think carefully about the potential impact of this on the partnership between parents and practitioners, asking the question of whose knowledge is given the greater legitimacy.

Working for integration

In the decade 1960–1970 the so-called *cultural revolution* in the West together with the expansion of childcare policies brought about changes in thinking and practice in early education and care. These were the heady days of widespread cultural and civil controversies. It was the period of the Vietnam War, the hippie and black power movements, feminist and student campaigns and a prelude to the end of apartheid in South Africa. It was a time of hope, of optimism – as the world seemed to be questioning the status quo and society in general began to recognise the danger of allowing the supremacy of the Western white race, of adults and men to continue without challenge. Significantly Sweden was the first country to establish a gender equality policy in1968 and the Scandinavian countries began a long programme to re-orient childcare and education by public investment. Many would claim that it was the role of the women's movement that brought about the new concept of *childcare*. Some see this as the precursor of what we now call early childhood education and care. In the new integrated or single provision childcare was to be an educational non-philanthropic service that was to be seen as a right – a right of children, women and families.

 Do you believe that this is, or should be, a right for all?

You can read more about this in Lenira Haddad's (2006) excellent paper 'Integrated Policies for Early Childhood Education and Care: Challenges, Pitfalls and Possibilities'.

From separate to integrated provision

Lenira Haddad is a significant figure in the ECECfSSW world and said that the legitimisation of what she calls *out-of-home socialising* is highly significant and it is rather difficult to understand why that should be. What exactly does she mean by out-of-home socialising? In split provision it is obvious that some children will be in education settings while others are in care settings. In education settings the focus will be on learning, and in care settings the focus on care. In reality all children need both care and education whatever age they are, whatever homes they live in. In a word it is a divided and divisive system. Where care and education are integrated, however, all the children are in the same place and so have the opportunity to mix with a more diverse group of peers. Children who are in integrated provision have more opportunities to have interactions with children both like them and different from them. In this way they will encounter different lifestyles, belief systems, ways of communicating, languages, cultures and customs. They are enriched by this. There is some evidence that where provision has been integrated the image of the young child will have been redefined. In short, in integrated settings all children whether poor, frail, troubled or rich, confident and integrated are regarded as complex, competent, communicative and complete individuals.

Yoshie Kaga, John Bennet and Peter Moss (2010), in their very detailed analysis of the integration of care and education in early childhood settings, looked at five areas: (1) concepts and processes; (2) assessing the impact of integration in education; (3) potential benefits; (4) potential drawbacks; and (5) the relative merits of integration in education or elsewhere.

It is important to note that integration is not a simple combining of two very different settings but a re-consideration of beliefs, values, needs, philosophy and practice. Issues to consider will be multiple and range from the simple to the complex. For example, do all staff need to have teaching qualifications or do no staff need teaching qualifications? How long should the day be? Do the babies need to be kept separate from the 5year olds? Should the integrated setting be the responsibility of welfare or education? Kaga *et al.* tell us that *'Integration is therefore better understood not as a state – either achieved or not – but as a continuum, ranging from minimal to full integration'* (2010: 12). We are told that integration is not a magic solution but a reform that can be both beneficial and dangerous. One danger is what some call the 'schoolification' of the offer to children and the lurking risk of them being 'taught' rather than being allowed to make and share meaning with others. There are also serious issues around the education and training, pay and conditions of staff. Finland is an example of a country that has adopted a Nordic welfare system, which includes a combination of free market capitalism with a comprehensive welfare state and collective bargaining at the national level. Care/welfare shares a number of key principles with education. These include universal access and the importance of learning; welfare systems in other countries do not generally focus on these aspects, making them less suitable locations for an integrated ECCE. The question of whether the education sector can provide a supportive environment for family day care (a form of individual ECCE provision where an individual carer provides for a small number of children in her own home) depends on how education is understood and the capacity of education to think more broadly.

Lenira Haddad had been influenced by the work of Uri Bronfenbrenner (1979) with his ecological model of human development. Ecological means being about or concerned

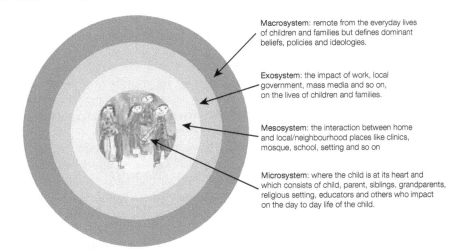

Figure 7.1 Bronfenbrenner's ecological model
Source: Smidt (2009: 44–45).

with the relation of living organisms to one another and to their physical surroundings. Those of you familiar with the work of Bronfenbrenner will recognise something of his model, which is often conceived of as a series of concentric circles (Figure 7.1). In this model the child is at the centre and around the child is a *microsystem* made up of the home, in which are the child, parents and, possibly, siblings; the religious setting, in which are the child, peers and adults; the school or setting, in which are the child, educators and peers; and the neighbourhood, in which are the child, adults and peers. The first concentric circle describes the *mesosystem*, which defines the interactions between home, school, neighbourhood and religious settings. Next is the *exosystem*, describing the impact (real or potential) of local industry, parents' workplaces, local government, mass media and school or setting/school management committee. Finally, and most remote from the child, are the *macrosystems*, which define the dominant beliefs and ideologies operating for that child and her family. Into this come things like laws. Bronfenbrenner later added the *chronosystem*, which relates to time and comes into play with regard to transitions from one stage or place.

Integrating care and education in Jamaica

As you can imagine, the process of integrating care and education in early childhood provision is immensely complicated and requires years of planning, evaluation, advocacy, research and consultation. I offer, as an example, the case of how this was achieved in Jamaica.

In 1993 early childcare and early education were separate with childcare being the responsibility of the Ministry of Health and early childhood education being the responsibility of the Ministry of Education. In that same year there had been an evaluation of day care services for the Ministry of Health and funded by UNICEF. Two years later in 1995 a similar evaluation was made of early childhood education by the Ministry of Education and funded by the Bernard van Leer Foundation. The two reports resulted in the <u>decision to move to integrating the two services</u>. This all took place at the time of UNICEF being very involved with examining the role of government departments in early childhood provision. In February 1995 a conference on early childhood took place and UNICEF made public its feelings about what they called the fragmentation of services. An Integration Task Force was set up consisting of people from the key ministries, the NGOs, international funding partners, many participants from the previous conference and others. This body was determined to <u>take account of the UN Convention on the Rights of the Child</u>, which Jamaica had ratified in 1993. Particular attention was to be paid to Articles 6 and 24, which state that <u>good early childhood care and education should provide much more than a school readiness programme for 0–6 year olds. They should address health and well-being, partnerships with parents, connections to other interested agencies, and examine accepted and valued educational practice and techniques, and competing ideas on child development</u>. The Task Force was guided by a UNICEF commissioned concept paper written by Dr Kerida McDonald. All this took place at the same time as a government programme to eradicate poverty and examine the role of early childhood education in regard to poverty. The Caribbean Plan of Action for Early Childhood Care, Education and Development was endorsed at a regional conference and adopted by various heads of state in 1997. There were significant developments in the world of early childhood education and care that followed – looking at the training of professionals in the field, setting up of a resource centre and a programme of sensitising key people in the Ministries about the significance and potential in quality provision.

Note: the underlined text shows the stages taken to integrate provision.

In integrating early childhood care and education, Jamaica faced big challenges since they started their reforms relatively recently and, to begin with, had deeply split systems. They also had significantly fewer resources than many richer countries. So it is remarkable how much progress they made by undertaking curricular and regulatory integration and by upgrading the workforce. Many people think that locating the responsibility for ECCE within education was important as the education framework highlights vital issues such as access, affordability, concern for a reasonably well-trained workforce and the existence of a curriculum as a basic tool for practice. Experts and researchers are reassuring in telling us that, except in one country, there is no evidence that integration within education has brought about 'schoolification' of ECCE services.

 What do you understand by schoolification and what do you think would be essential for integration to be successful?

It seems likely that in future, early childhood settings will be integrated rather than separated into care and education and in order for this to function the following are essential:

- A clearer definition of what is meant when we talk of state (or public) and family (or private) responsibilities, roles and relationships concerning children's affairs.
- An explicit recognition of the social, cultural and intellectual rights of the child to be cared for and socialised in a context wider than that of the family alone.

- A similar recognition of the right of the family to share the care and education of the child with society.
- A commitment to recognising that childcare is a professional task which, together with education, can promote the child's full development.
- An undertaking that staff, both male and female, at all levels in the setting will be qualified and well-paid professionals, with clearly defined roles and good working conditions.
- A commitment to valuing parental and community involvement so that culture and language are explicitly recognised and celebrated.
- Last and most important, a determination that each child is viewed as a competent, capable, communicative citizen of her community.

Some sustainable projects: who is leading?

Case Study 9: Save water

Julie Davis, whose work we touched on earlier in the book, described projects around sustainability that were developed at a long day-care centre known as Campus Kindergarten in Australia. The centre caters for children aged between the ages of 2 and 5. In her piece called 'What might education for sustainability look like in early childhood?' in Pramling Samuelsson and Kaga (2008) she wrote about how the children became able to initiate projects for sustainability themselves. Initially the children were invited to develop mini projects and the pedagogy was teacher-initiated with children following. But as time passed, these mini-projects – such as litter-less lunches or frog pond or responsible cleaning – simply became embedded into the everyday practices of the centre.

What happened next was that the children themselves became the inventors or initiators of new projects. This is a brief account of one such child-initiated project. It concerns water conservation.

There was, as there often is in that region, a severe drought. The children and the adults noticed that they were all using water carelessly by doing things like pouring more water into their glasses than they could drink and then tipping the rest onto the garden. From this initial observation, a whole centre project about water conservation emerged. Based on what the children had observed, related to their life experiences of living in a place where water is precious and sometimes rare, the children were able to express their concerns. In doing this they were effectively leading what happened. It required collaboration between children, parents and teachers to become a centre-wide project. Remember that these are young children – most of them aged around 4. They talked about what they could do and how they could do it and who would do what and how they could tell others of their findings. They became little researchers. The teachers were, of course, involved in supporting the children by listening to them, answering their questions, offering resources, helping find evidence or information. The children raised some difficult and complex questions, wanting to know how the water gets into the taps in their homes and nursery, what exactly a drought is and what causes it. And as the children's knowledge of water issues increased their questions became actions.

Three children, Mia, Layla and Andrew, made informative signs based on what they had considered and learned.

Mia's sign said: Please don't leave the tap running.
Layla's sign said: When you flush the toilet, press the small button.
Andrew's sign was: Turn the hose off when you are finished.
The project even crept into the homes of the children, as one parent told staff:
The water issue . . . he's bringing it into bath time. We're only allowed to fill the bath to a
certain level and we're not allowed to put the tap on again!

(Davis 2008: 21–22)

You can read more about Campus Kindergarten later in the book.

Case Study 10: EducaT Hilo in Cuba

It is extraordinary that 70% of Cuban children under the age of 6 participate in EducaT Hilo, which is a non-institutionalised, multi-sector, community-based programme to educate preschool children. It is run by the Ministry of Education, which puts the family at the centre of activities. The aim of the scheme is to ensure that young children achieve the best levels in terms of emotional communication, language, motor skills, health, nutrition and more. The starting point of the programme required that the parents lead it. In theory the programme was managed by promoters who might have been teachers, educators or health professionals and who acted as liaison between a local coordinating group and the community. Their role was to educate the community, mobilise resources, train facilitators and provide pedagogical guidance according to the plans drawn up by the programme's coordinating groups. The programme works with two age groups: The first is for children from birth to 2 and the second from 2 to 6.

- The babies' group gets individual care from the facilitators who visit their homes once or twice a week. This at-home session consists of demonstrations of 'stimulation activities' by the facilitators, modelling this for the parents. The content will vary according to the needs of the children and their parents.
- The group of older children participate with their parents or carers in group sessions held once or twice a week in a community space such as a park or sports or cultural centre. The groups may be broken down into age groups and at least one family member who has been trained in the home session and group sessions attends.

I can just picture some raised eyebrows but like everything this has to be understood in context. In this socialist country children and families are not alone: they are backed up by the community. Social cohesion is really significant and means that children grow up with a sense of social responsibility because child development is a shared responsibility. What a lovely thought that is!

The programme has been in operation for almost 20 years and is being replicated in Brazil and Ecuador and other Latin American countries are considering its implementation. It made me think and I hope it has the same effect on you (Tinajero, A. (2010). Scaling up Early Childhood Development in Cuba. Wolfensohn Centre for Development Working Paper no. 16. www.brookings.adu/papers/20/10/04_child_development_cuba_tinajeo.aspx).

Moving on . . .

In this chapter there were many issues to be considered, primarily whether it is possible to just educate or just care for very young children or whether all provision should be integrated. Some of this has been contentious and some difficult to understand but in the next chapter we talk about the role of culture in our lives and in the task of tackling sustainability.

Chapter 8

Cultural considerations

Key words and concepts: making culture; passing it on; changing it; cultural resilience; cultural identity; cultural heritage; cultural practices; stereotypes; global perspective; see through the eyes of others; guided participation; learning by doing; respect; bias; prejudice; change society; empathy; planet awareness; respect for cultural differences; technology.

You may recall from the first chapter that the three pillars of education for sustainable development in the early years are thought to be *society, environment and economy*, all underpinned by culture.

It is complex to define culture because it refers to so many things. Everyone holds a common-sense definition of culture in their heads. This mainly refers to the beliefs, artefacts, values and other things that bind people together. These may be the music, the food, the language(s), religion(s), customs and clothing that make people feel a sense of belonging to the group. This is rather a superficial definition and ignores the role played by the players in *making culture* and *passing it on* and *changing it*. That definition makes it seem that culture is something fixed and 'given' to those born into it rather than seeing its dynamic nature. Culture, like language, changes with usage and over time. The cultural theorist Stuart Hall said that

> *People who are in any way different from the majority – 'them' rather than us' – are frequently exposed to binary extremes – good/bad, civilised/primitive, ugly/excessively attractive, repelling-because-different/compelling because strange and exotic. And they are often required to be both things at the same time.*

(1992: 17)

 What are the implications of this for children?

Since we are social beings our children live in communities and within our communities there are different cultures. Children are constantly being defined by others – often negatively – and very possibly on the basis of their class or religion, their gender or their physical features, their race or their language. We know that children construct their own identities from their experiences and through their interactions with others. The ways in which they and other members of their groups are represented will be crucial in doing this. Identity construction is a complex process and depends to a large extent on self-esteem. A child with low self-esteem is one who will be more easily teased or ignored. If you are interested in this I recommend you read a very old but wonderful book called *Minority Education: From Shame to Struggle* (Skutnabb-Kangas & Cummins), which was written in 1988 and is sadly still relevant. In terms of thinking about sustainability it is important that young children are educated to have respect for groups other than their own and a recognition that not all children live as they do.

Cultural heritage: cultural resilience

In a UNESCO *Global Report on Culture for Sustainability* (2016) Hamady Bocoum, the Director General of the Musée des Civilisations Noires (Museum of Black Civilisations) in Dakar (Senegal), wrote the following passage:

> *Cultural development is probably the greatest challenge for the sustainability of our cities. A culture of sustainable development implies the existence of a genuine policy that promotes diversity and good practices. For developing countries, culture can become the foundation of sustainable development within the framework of an urbanisation that concerns people and their environment.*
>
> (2016: 41)

Bocoum was writing expressly about cities and didn't mention children, old or young. His focus was on black civilisations in Africa. Yet what he says has significance for us all. His primary argument is that valuing and celebrating what has already been invented, created, made or developed by people acting together should be protected and preserved. This is what he calls *cultural resilience* – a culture's ability to maintain and develop cultural identity and critical cultural knowledge and practices.

⁇ How would you define cultural identity and cultural knowledge and practices?

Cultural identity is the feeling of belonging to a group or identifying with a group. It is part of a person's self-conception and self-perception and may be related to nationality, ethnicity, religion, social class, generation, locality or any kind of social group that has its own distinct culture.

This is how I might define my cultural identity: '*I am South African and British, white, atheist and culturally Jewish, socialist, middle class, divorced, graduate, privileged, woman, old, a mother and grandmother, sister and aunt, a friend and a colleague, an educator and a writer, an amateur painter and viola player.*'

Cultural identity is how we define where we think we belong in terms of our culture. Everyone will define their cultural identity differently. My cultural knowledge is what I have come to know through my experience, education, opportunities, relationships and values.

Cultural practices are how groups display aspects of their cultures – for example the ways in which they mark important dates like birthdays or religious dates; ceremonies like births, deaths, marriage, starting school, graduation and so on.

Belonging

It is obvious that young children become part of their culture from birth. They are inducted into the activities and values of those closest to them through their interactions first with the primary caregiver, who is usually the mother. Colwyn Trevarthen and now many others believe that the human infant is born *purposive* in becoming a member of her family, community and culture. He arrived at this conclusion as a result of his close and in-depth analysis of film clips of newborns and their mothers and/or fathers where he noted that when the baby is rested and alert and in the company of those who are clearly sympathetic to her, the actions and gestures and vocalisations she makes invite positive responses from the mother/father. The consequence is that the mother or father has an immediate sense of interacting with a little human person. Each of these interactions takes place within a context – a context that is not only physical but also cultural. Every baby is born into some culture in terms of language, customs, beliefs, rituals, history, artefacts and more. The mother vocalises; the baby listens and hears and vocalises back. In response the mother, perhaps, says something in the language of the culture. The baby listens, hears and vocalises back. Trevarthen called these exchanges protoconversation. He also said that the human infant is interested in the companionship of others and, over time, as she engages with others not only in protoconversations but also in sharing objects, songs, games and rituals – all of which are particular to her culture – she gains a sense of pride in belonging to a family and a culture.

You have only to think about how mothers and others sing to babies in almost every culture throughout the world or notice how intently a baby watches what others are doing to understand the beginnings of becoming part of a culture. You may have come across the work of Barbara Rogoff who argued that human development must be understood as a cultural process, not simply a biological or psychological one. Individuals develop as members of a community, and their development can only be fully understood by examining the practices and circumstances of their communities. In her book *Apprenticeship in Thinking* (1990) she talked of how young children, treated as members of their culture, do what they see more experienced others doing and then join in. This *guided participation* explains how more experienced members of groups induct the youngest and least skilled members of the community into some activity first by talking about what is being done and then inviting the child to join in. In other words the young child is *learning by doing*. In essence children participate in the cultural activities of their elders when these activities match their own initiative and skills.

Case Study 11: Weaving in Guatemala and knowing which hand does what in India

- A group of women are sitting in the courtyard chatting and weaving whilst two little girls watch them. Saria, aged 5, surprises them all by setting up her own loom and playing with some strips of thread that she finds lying around. She manages to plait a long 'leaf' of these threads but then gets tired and gives up.
- Anoop is with his mother who is teaching him the correct use of his left and right hands. The custom in his Indian village is to use the right or 'clean' hand for eating and the left or 'dirty' hand to wipe himself after defecation.

Learning to resist bias in Liberia

Liberia is on the west coast of Africa and was ranked as one of the poorest countries in the world. Then it faced the devastating outbreak of the Ebola virus in 2014, which led to 4,809 deaths. As you can imagine this significantly weakened its already vulnerable healthcare system, and effectively halted progress across all social sector domains. Despite this, Liberia made notable gains on some of the Millennium Development Goals: it even surpassed the target for reducing child mortality and made great progress on gender equality. And, in still difficult circumstances, the country is steadily making progress in developing an enabling environment for young children. Liberia's recent efforts to build an early childhood development system began in 2007/8 when the country was emerging from a brutal civil and regional war. The fact that the government recognised early on the importance of investing in its youngest citizens to start rebuilding its society and economy led them to recognise and more importantly address two big challenges: a general lack of awareness about the benefits of investing in young children, and the lack of a skilled workforce. Hawa Kamara wrote a chapter called 'Early childhood education for a sustainable society' (2008) and it is such a hopeful and life-affirming piece that I take the liberty of quoting from it since Kamara's voice is so much more powerful than mine. Here she talks about building a self-image:

 Why is having a positive self-image important for young children learning about sustainability?

The early years are the time to begin helping children to form strong, positive self-images and grow up to respect and get along with people who are different from themselves. We know from research that children between 2 and 5 start becoming aware of gender, race, ethnicity, and disabilities. They also begin to absorb both the positive attitudes and negative biases attached to these aspects of our identity by family members and other significant adults in their lives. If we want children to like themselves and value diversity, we must learn how to help them resist the biases and prejudices that are still far too prevalent in our world. Bias based on gender, race, disability, or social class creates serious obstacles to all young children's healthy development. In order to develop healthy self-esteem, they must learn how to interact fairly and productively with different types of people. Naturally, children's curiosity will lead them to ask questions: 'Why is her skin so dark?' 'Why does he speak funny?' We may hide our own negative feelings, or hope that children simply will not notice, but our avoidance actually teaches children that some differences are not acceptable. We must face our own biased attitudes and change them in order to help foster all children's growth. The most dangerous is race segregation.

(2008: 104)

Kamara goes on to remind us of what parents and teachers can do:

- *Recognise that because we live in a world where many biases exist, we must counteract them – or else we will support them through our silence.*
- *At home or at school, give children messages that deliberately contrast stereotypes by providing books, dolls, toys, wall decorations, television programmes, and records that show: (a) men and women in non-traditional roles; (b) people of different colour in leadership positions; (c) people with disabilities doing activities familiar to children; and (d) various types of families and family activities.*

- *Show no bias in the friends, doctors, teachers, and other service providers that you choose, or in the stores where you shop. Remember what you do is as important as what you say.*
- *Make it a firm rule that a person's appearance is never an acceptable reason for teasing or rejecting them. Immediately step in if you hear or see your child behave in such a way.*
- *Talk positively about each child's physical characteristics and cultural heritage.*
- *Help children learn the differences between feelings of superiority and those of self-esteem and pride in their own heritage.*
- *Provide opportunities for children to interact with other children who are racially/culturally different from themselves, and with people who have various disabilities.*
- *Respectfully listen to and answer children's questions about themselves and others. Do not ignore, change the subject, or in any way make the child think she is bad for asking such a question.*
- *Teach children how to challenge biases about who they are. Give them tools to confront those who act biased against them.*
- *Use accurate and fair images in contrast to stereotypes, and encourage children to talk about the differences.*
- *Help them to think critically about what they see in books, films, greeting cards, comics, and on television.*
- *Let children know that unjust things can be changed. Encourage children to challenge bias, and involve children in taking action on issues relevant to their lives. Building a healthy self-identity is a process that continues all our lives. Help children get a head start by teaching them to resist bias, and to value the differences between people as much as the similarities.*

(104–105)

I really hope that you can 'hear' Kamara's voice and that you, like me, think this advice to be essential for anyone interested in society, justice, diversity and equity.

 Why is having a positive self-image important for young children learning about sustainability? Read on to help you think about this question.

Some basic concepts of early childhood global education for sustainability

Douglas Bell, Raynice E. Jean-Sigur and Yanghee A. Kim (2015) decided that there were six basic concepts of early childhood global education for us to consider. These are: perspective consciousness, cross-cultural awareness, state of the planet awareness, system connectedness, awareness and utilisation of technology and options for participation. All are concerned with culture.

In any book on early childhood education for a sustainable future it is obviously important to consider issues that apply to all the countries in the world: in other words to adopt a *global perspective*. It is evident that, in order to address sustainability, we must also consider how to *change society* in order to deal with the consequences of our past and present behaviour. Global education is said to be a creative approach of bringing about change in our society. Any successful early childhood programme should offer active learning through play and experimentation and be based on the universal values of tolerance, solidarity, equality, justice, inclusion, co-operation and non-violence.

The concepts are as follows.

The first concept states that **children need to become able to see things through the eyes of another**. In education this is sometimes called the ability to *decentre* - which means developing the sensitivity to be able to see things not only from one's own perspective but to see things as others do. It has to do with not needing to be central to everything and being able to demonstrate empathy. Some theorists question whether young children are capable of doing this but you have only to think of what happens when one child sees another cut her knee or get into trouble for something she did not do. Living in a family, in a neighbourhood, in a village or a city, almost all children grow up alongside others. Being able to decentre is essential to being able to function in society. How we see one another may be largely determined by nationality, ethnicity, religion, culture, class, age, gender and social status. And it is all too evident that how we see one another may be biased, prejudiced and stereotypical. But let's remind ourselves that we are all citizens of the same world and have to find ways to help young children adopt a global perspective which is devoid of negative thinking about 'others'.

There is a strong consensus that educating for sustainability should begin very early in life. It is in the early childhood period that children develop their basic values, attitudes, skills, behaviours and habits, which may be long lasting. Studies have shown that racial stereotypes are learned early and that young children are able to pick up cultural messages about wealth and inequality. As early childhood education is about laying a sound intellectual, psychological, emotional, social and physical foundation for development and lifelong learning, it has an enormous potential in fostering values, attitudes, skills and behaviours that support sustainable development. We need to ensure we develop the wise use of resources, cultural diversity, gender equality and democracy.

 Suppose you had a little girl with wonderful black tightly curled hair in your group who is being called 'weird' and teased by the other children. How would you handle this for the benefit of both the little girl and the group teasing her?

There are many possible solutions including talking to the children; inviting them to draw one another; celebrating what is the same, what is similar, what is different. It is all about acknowledging and celebrating diversity. Finding story books that include a range of characters is always a good ploy.

The second concept is referred to as **cross-cultural awareness, which merely means knowing that we are all the same in some ways and all different in others**. We are all of the same species so most of us have two arms, two legs, two eyes, two ears. Some of us have blue eyes and others brown eyes. Some have pink skin and others brown. Some like potatoes and others rice. Now in order to develop an awareness of and respect for our own culture and that of others, we have to consider and develop a number of things, including the following:

- a sense of who is like us and shares our values and beliefs;
- an awareness that other people have their own culture, values and beliefs;
- how to show respect for the views and values of others and not simplify these in order to creates stereotypes; and learn positive ways of interacting with others.

Many people grow up never having learned the skill of relating positively with people different from themselves. I grew up in apartheid South Africa where park and street benches were reserved for white people and were labelled with signs saying '*Slegs Blankes*', which means 'only white people'. Black people lived in townships on the fringes of cities and did menial work. Hatred flourished. It was a poisonous place in which to live and I was lucky to have had educated parents who operated as citizens of the world. Those working as carers and educators in early childhood have very significant roles in regard to this because globalisation has meant that many populations in the world are made up of different communities, cultures, languages, beliefs, religions and customs. This is a richness and good early childcare professionals will know this and be able to support young children experience and enjoy diversity. How lucky they are to be able to dance to Indian music, eat Turkish bread, dress in saris, wear cowboy hats, hear stories from Russia, use chopsticks in the home corner, hear different languages and much more.

 How might you approach doing this within an ECEC setting?

It seems unnecessary to say much other than to suggest you read Kamara's words of advice to practitioners quoted earlier in this chapter.

The third concept is **state of the planet awareness** or *It's our earth: let's take care of it*. Many young children are interested in the natural world they inhabit. They are enchanted by the sun and moon and stars, accustomed to being outdoors as well as indoors. They are interested in who they share the planet with – all sorts of people and animals and insects and plants. They ask questions about the world and the natural phenomena they encounter. In many settings there is space outdoors to grow things and, in some places, pets to care for. Many, but certainly not all, children can play in fields or parks. No one wants to terrify young children by telling them that the world is going to end but they do need to come to understand that some of the things that they and those close to them do as part of everyday life damage the earth. Many of the programmes in early childhood settings are concerned about pollution, saving water, how to get rid of unwanted things, and caring for plants and animals. This makes this concept the easiest for early childhood practitioners to deal with. Many nursery classes collect empty containers, waste paper, bits of left over fabric, for the children to use when making things. Often there is a class pet to care for. Things get thrown away at the end of the day and some settings help the children learn to recycle. And many settings encourage children to adopt something – perhaps a tree or a rabbit or chicken or a plant which needs to be tended.

 How might you approach doing this within an ECEC setting?

The extract below comes from a piece on the role of early childhood education in establishing a sustainable society, written by Siren Qemuge (in Pramling Samuelsson and Yoshie Kaga 2008). It relates to Urad Front Banner, a small, poverty-stricken town in Inner Mongolia in North Central China. The region is afflicted by the rapid desertification of the grasslands, which causes sandstorms and other natural disasters.

Case Study 12: Creating a democratic environment and respect for individual cultural differences

Here is what Siren Qemuge says about this issue:

Culture is public behaviour that must be for the good of all. We can say with some certainty that it is through the flow of behaviour (or more precisely, social action), that cultural forms find articulation. Our preschool is not only available for our Mongolian minority group, but also for the Chinese (Han) and Muslim children as well. The different ethnic groups found amongst the children use the Mongolian or Chinese language to communicate, thereby using multiple cultural environments to meet and be able to communicate with different people. This strengthens their positive attitudes towards more cosmopolitan lifestyles.

(2008: 84)

In addition, schools and nurseries encourage children to wear different national clothes on special days to celebrate the festivals; Han, Muslim and Mongolian children learn to play, dance and have some special food together. There is the playing of a kind of gymnastics with chopsticks taken from Mongolian traditional dancing; trying out physical wrestling games, which are a Mongolian cultural activity. In such activities it is believed that the children come to understand the cultures of others. This is especially important for some Mongolian children who have lived in the remote mountainous regions with no chance to play with other children but have had to make do with lambs, calves and puppies, and whose environment is being daily ravaged and destroyed. When the children participate in activities like these they are bound to communicate with one another.

The piece ends with this warning: '*At the same time, their love of animals, nature, independence and bravery can greatly influence some of the other children who have been spoiled by their parents too much in town*' (2008: 84).

The fourth concept is called **system connectedness**, which really just means the interactions between societies, cultures and subcultures. To understand this, think about the model of society provided by Bronfenbrenner, cited earlier. You will remember that his ecological model went from the intimate unit of the family to the remote unit of the state. Good early childhood practitioners know that young children may already know a great deal about the family and the intimate and almost nothing about the state and remote. All learning starts with what is already known or is of interest to the learner. This is often called *developmentally appropriate practice*. I like to think of it as learning through what interests or concerns the child and this requires practitioners to be truly attentive to what the children, as individuals, are questioning or seeking. Going from the *close to the far* means that young children come to know that we interact with, rely on, and learn from others – and these others may not be quite like us. Good practitioners will already be thinking about activities, building the classroom culture and promoting activities that require children to work with one another.

 How might you approach doing this within an ECEC setting? Read the extract below and decide if you consider it something worth striving to emulate:

In their paper called 'A Comparison of the National Preschool Curricula in Norway and Sweden' in ECRP 1(2) 1999, Alvestad and Pramling Samuelsson, both highly respected writers on many aspects of early childhood education and care and also on sustainability, tell us that, in the curriculum in Swedish preschools, allowing children to have an influence on their everyday life in preschool is a specific goal. To achieve this, each preschool should try to give every child every opportunity to develop the following abilities to:

- express her thoughts and opinions in order to influence her life decisions and choices;
- take responsibility not only for her own actions but also for the environment of the preschool;
- understand and act in accordance with democratic principles by being involved in different forms of cooperation and decision-making processes.
- develop openness, respect, solidarity and responsibility;
- respect and understand other human beings, their cultures, languages, customs and situations;
- discover, reflect upon and be able to express her opinion on what might be seen as ethical dilemmas and issues of everyday life;
- understand that all people have equal worth, independent of gender, age, capacity and social or ethnic background;
- develop and behave with respect for all living species and care for our environment.

And throughout, cooperation with parents is an absolute necessity.

(based on Alvestad & Pramling Samuelson, 1999)

The fifth concept is **awareness and use of technology – or let's get connected**. Very young children are accustomed to and at ease with a world that has been digital for all of their lives. There are those educationalist who may be wary and sceptical of the advantages of encouraging digital proficiency in young children but the reality is that they imitate what they have seen done and so learn to access undreamed of worlds. Siraj-Blatchford and Whitebread (2003: 6) said that

> the use of ICT in the early years has the potential to enhance educational opportunities for young children. It can be applied in a developmentally appropriate manner to encourage purposeful and exploratory play. It can encourage discussion, creativity, problem solving, risk taking and flexible thinking, and this can all be achieved in a play-centred and responsive environment. However, all of this does demand that practitioners are well trained and skilled in the appropriate uses of ICT with young children.

 How might you approach doing this within an ECEC setting?

I imagine that some of you reading this will have reservations in terms of how you can scaffold young children's use of technology but there are resources you can find and things you can do. I came across *ePals* and went to their website and was delighted to find that some of it is very concerned about sustainability and interested in how to attempt to deal with it. For example there is *Invent It*, which is an annual competition that inspires students around the world to, as the website puts it, *unleash their inner inventor*. Using *Smithsonian's Spark!Lab Invention Process*, students brainstorm new inventions to solve global problems.

Go online and follow this link: http://americanhistory.si.edu/exhibitions/sparklab. Here you can find details and follow the instructions. For the 2017 Challenge, participants were asked to focus their minds and talents on generating new solutions to environmental problems such as water scarcity, climate change, air pollution, water pollution, endangered species, invasive species and natural resource loss. It is not aimed at the youngest children but those aged 5–7 can enter either individually or in collaboration with others. They can then submit a slide show or video presentation of an invention or idea that solves an environmental problem, as well as the process used to develop it. They will use their own digital skills to find out more.

The sixth and last concept is that **we all play our part**. I don't propose to write much about this because basically it means joining in with others of all ages in activities focused on the sustainability of our planet. In a brain-storming session with some students, we came up with the list of possible collaborative activities as serious citizens in the search for sustainable projects.

 How might you approach doing this within an ECEC setting?

These are the suggestions of the students: add your own.

- A no-trash lunch.
- A day when everyone brings in something healthy to share with a friend.
- Arrange a collection of spare coins – perhaps from holidays abroad – and donate them to *Change for Good* (United Nations International Children's Emergency Fund).
- Have a sandwich-making activity involving children and parents and take them to a local soup kitchen.
- Invite parents to come in and cook something healthy for the children.
- Convert part of the playground into a garden in which to grow vegetables.
- Talk to the children about how they can use waste materials and turn that into a project.
- Adopt a tree.
- Adopt a pet.
- Get each child to draw or paint a portrait of another child and select one who is different in some way. At the end, display a collage made up of the different portraits with a suitable title – *We are all friends* or *We are all different*. Or your own title or one suggested by the children.
- Talk to the children about how they can collect and save water.

Moving on . . .

You have been reading about culture and why it is something that has to be taken serious account of in considering how to educate our children for sustainability. And now, to quote Monty Python, for something completely different.

Chapter 9

Other ways of thinking

Key words and concepts: environmental modelling; ecological footprint; interdisciplinary research; ecosystem; regenerative; consuming resources from the earth; environmental impact of human behaviour; transformative learning; cradle-to-cradle thinking; capitalism, business and the market.

While researching for this book I came across an article in a journal entitled *Environmental Education Research* and, as it had the words <u>early childhood</u> and <u>sustainability</u> in the title, I thought it might be relevant. And it was not only relevant but a revelation. It was written by Heidi McNichol who is an engineer in the coal industry, Julie Davis who is a lecturer with a long history in advocating for the inclusion of early childhood education for sustainability on early childhood teacher education programmes and Katherine O'Brien who is a lecturer in environmental education and conducts research in the area of environmental modelling and whose children went to the Campus Kindergarten, the subject of this paper. The title of the paper is as unexpected as the career paths of the authors: 'An ecological footprint for an early learning centre: Identifying opportunities for early childhood sustainability education through interdisciplinary research' (2011).

I am sure that you know what an ecological footprint is but just in case here are one or two definitions:

- It is the impact of human activities measured in terms of the area of biologically productive land and water required to produce the goods consumed and to assimilate the wastes generated.
- It is the impact of a person or community on the environment, expressed as the amount of land required to sustain their use of natural resources.

The education and career paths of the authors can guarantee we are looking at a piece of <u>interdisciplinary research</u>.

Quantifying the problem

By now we should all be aware of the aspects of our lives that threaten the survival of this planet. McNichol, Davis and O'Brien (2011) tell us that our current rates of resource consumption are unsustainable. More than that the amount of land we use to provide goods and services is damaging the earth and depleting what the authors call our 'natural capital'. This is our world's stocks of natural assets, which include geology, soil, air, water and all living things. It is from this natural capital that humans derive a wide range of services, often called <u>ecosystem services</u>, which make human life on earth possible. These include the production of food and the protection of the quality water. The ecological footprint can give us an indication of just how much regenerative (things that can revive) biological capacity is being used by us and that tells us where consumption exceeds the environmental limits both nationally or globally. It might help to know that bio-capacity refers to the capacity of a given biologically productive area to generate an ongoing or never ending supply of renewable resources and to absorb its spillover wastes. Un-sustainability occurs if the area's ecological footprint exceeds its bio-capacity. A frightening fact is that in 2003 the global ecological footprint found that the use of land by humans exceeded the earth's bio-capacity by 27%. This is technical, statistical and a little frightening. But we all know that if we don't change our lifestyles we will not have a planet fit for our children and for their children.

Put more simply, we can say that we humans are biological beings, and part of the ecology on earth. We have been using resources from the earth to live on and survive, grow, develop and expand our civilisations for generations. Every individual and community on earth, from the beginning of time, has been consuming resources from the earth in order to grow. So an ecological footprint simply means the impact of human activities on the globe and the amount of resources necessary to produce the goods and services necessary to support a particular lifestyle, in terms of the area of biologically productive land and water. The footprint also measures how m resource is needed to produce what we need, and what we consume and dispose of.

It seems apparent that the use of the ecological footprint has not been widely used in considerations of sustainability at the early childhood level and the research team involved in this project believed that this was not only possible but necessary. To understand this you just have to keep reading. Keep in mind that the purpose of the study was to discover how to reduce the environmental impact of what was being done at the kindergarten now and in the future.

'Saving our planet: become a conscious part of the solution'

Campus Kindergarten (CK) is situated on land leased from The University of Queensland. The central structure of the kindergarten is the original cottage once belonging to the caretaker of the University. Some years later the University moved the cottage from its old site to its present day location. The kindergarten was originally designed to accommodate 36 children aged between 2 and 5 years old. Now it has 73–76 children in the same age range. Obviously, as demand for places grew, so did the building with the addition of the pre-kindergarten room and its cool, wide verandahs. In late 1993, major renovations were carried out to comply with the new 1993 Child Care Centre Regulations.

Campus Kindergarten offers a seamless day from the morning through to 5.30 in the evening. It is described as being a community, not-for-profit organisation managed by a volunteer parent-committee or board of management. It is an integrated setting where education and care are both offered. Like many Australian settings it has been involved in the '*Sustainable Planet Project*', which, Julie Davis (2005) tells us, originated in 1997 and was the result of a staff team-building exercise to encourage home/work linkages in a long day care centre. In looking for a suitable shared project, '*the environment*' emerged as a common interest. What becoming involved in the project meant was that individual staff members were able to add value to their roles as early childhood educators and perhaps their own lives by including personal interests such as gardening, wildlife conservation and recycling. The project's subtitle was '*Saving our planet: become a conscious part of the solution*'.

That all sounds like the beginning of a happy story and some of the story is happy. The '*Saving our Planet*' project had been running for many years, yet, according to the researchers in this study, the kindergarten community had no quantitative measure of their environmental impacts. In other words, nobody had any idea of how successful or otherwise it has been in terms of sustainability.

Understanding the specific goals of this project

The three researchers (McNichol, Davis & O'Brien 2011), as you know, are not all early childhood experts but they are experts in sustainability, in the use of analytical tools to evaluate a project, and to apply their findings generally. They are looking for solutions that will apply to the whole sector of early childhood education and care. They summarised their objectives like this:

(1) We want to quantify the environmental impact of the kindergarten by working out its ecological footprint (which we defined earlier in this chapter).
(2) We also want to identify what main things contribute to the impact of the ecological footprint as well as working out how the kindergarten might reduce this impact.
(3) Then we will use the calculations of the footprint to gain more understanding of how we might be able reduce the environmental impact across the whole early childhood sector and do this through considering the design and the management of early years settings.
(4) Finally we plan to provide information and examples of how this can be incorporated into early childhood sustainability education.

In short, the broad scope of the project was to examine the lifecycle of all measurable goods and services consumed by the kindergarten within its grounds, including the impact of the transport of the children to and from the school, roughly over a year. The goods included electricity, water, food, waste, transport and paper.

Using the concept of global footprints in early childhood settings

The researchers came to the conclusion that each child's footprint amounted to 10 m × 10 m – which is 100 square metres. This is a vast footprint for one small child. They suggested that if you want to develop this into a project with the young children you work with, you might mark out, in the playground, the 'footprint' of one child and then get the other children to work with a friend to make one another's footprints. To work out a footprint you would need to consider the following six components: electricity, water, food, waste, transport and paper.

(1) It not only possible but likely that one can reduce the size of the footprint by thinking about the **food decisions made**. We know that what young children eat is largely determined by the parents of the children and there are sustainable decisions

that make sense. In many countries early childhood settings have made planting things and growing food part of the curriculum and have attempted to make gardens in which to grow vegetables or fruit or setting up chicken coops.

(2) **Transport decisions** are obviously not in the hands of the children but a project on walking to the kindergarten or riding your bike might spark off more ideas. Remember that sustainability means thinking ahead and the young children today are going to have to make transport decisions as they grow older.

(3) **Reducing the energy** footprint is a huge issue and can probably only be resolved by thinking about installing solar panels. This applies particularly in the planning of future early childhood settings. But the children can be involved in learning to conserve energy by turning things off and learning about how and why to save energy.

(4) **Water is often regarded as an essential resource** in early childhood settings and it is, of course, something that young children love to have available to explore. Again, staff should ensure that they talk to children about how precious it is so that children learn to turn off taps and don't pour water away. Do remember that what children learn in the setting is often taken home so that the children become advocates for what is good for sustainability.

(5) I was surprised to read that the **footprint of waste was not very worrying**. It appears that dealing with waste is something that today's adults are doing. Parents and children are more and more aware of the dangers of waste and engage in good practices. They follow the advice of reduce, reuse and recycle. In some places parents are encouraged to bring litter-less lunches for their children and children draw on both sides of the paper and everywhere has a place for recycling.

A learning experience of a different kind

Transformative Learning Theory, developed by Jack Mezirow (1991), introduced a new way of thinking about adult education. His thesis was that learning can be the process of using prior interpretation to develop and refine ideas, thoughts, experiences and actions. He was following in the steps of Habermas who talked of *instrumental learning*, which is learning to do, based on empirical/analytical discovery and *communicative learning*, which is learning involved in making sense of what others are conveying through their words and actions. Put more simply, Mezirow was saying that people can re-think big issues – sustainability, for example – by paying attention to what others say and then critically reflect on this. So it is a type of social and cultural learning. The power of the argument rests in the label 'transformative', which means just what it says – able to change. Based on a national study of women returning to college and attending a specially designed programme for those re-entering the profession, Mezirow decided that each person involved went through ten stages as follows:

(1) A disorientating dilemma.
(2) Self-examination associated with feelings of shame or guilt.
(3) A critical assessment of assumptions.
(4) The recognition that negative feelings associated with the whole process are shared by other participants.
(5) Exploration of options for possible new roles, relationships, actions.

(6) Planning a course of action.
(7) Acquiring new knowledge and skills matched to one's new plans.
(8) Trying out new roles.
(9) Building competence and self-confidence in new roles and relationships.
(10) A reintegration into one's life on the basis of conditions dictated by one's new perspective.

Mezirow was certain that there were three crucial features essential for the transformation of learning: critical reflection, centrality of experience and rational discourse. This is background to what follows, which would be hard to make sense of without a taste of transformative learning theory.

Education Is the Key to a Sustainable Future

Şebnem Feriver, Gaye (Tuncer) Teksöz, Refika Olgan and Alan Reid (2016) were members of staff in the Department of Elementary Education in Ankara in Turkey and eager to work with Turkish-speaking colleagues to enable them to successfully train early childhood teachers for sustainability. Having encountered the work of Mezirow they developed a small-scale project to evaluate an in-service or 'on the job' training programme that promised to offer what they said was a focus on *'perspective transformation' in early childhood education for sustainability* (2016: 717).

Twenty-four early childhood practitioners volunteered for the study. They were all working in public schools in a town in the north west of Turkey. The group was made up of 23 women plus 1one man. All were graduates and familiar with reflective practice, which, you remember, is where the child's interests or concerns are followed. None of the volunteers had any experience of early childhood education for sustainability in their regular work, or in teacher education or during in-service programmes. It was felt that this project, *Education Is the Key to a Sustainable Future*, was suitable for a Mezirow-style perspective transformation 'programme' because it was believed that the *developmentally appropriate practices* (DAP) in EfS and ECE had common characteristics.

 Do you know what developmentally appropriate practices are? And what features do they have in common?

DAP is said to be an approach to teaching grounded in both the research on how young children develop and learn and in what is known about effective early education. Like all programmes, it's aim is to promote young children's optimal learning and development. The features that are shared by early childhood education and early childhood education for sustainability are a focus on *direct experience* and *promoting the child to be able to follow up her own interests* and concerns rather than those of the teacher.

Feriver *et al.*'s (2016) project was very complex in design and built up of four sections:

(1) the state of the planet and lifestyle patterns;
(2) relations and networks as well as causes and effects, plus an introduction to cradle-to-cradle thinking*;
(3) sustainability, its integration into education and EfS projects; and
(4) the integration of sustainability into one's life.

Note: *Cradle-to-cradle is a biomimetic approach to the design of products and systems that models human industry on nature's processes, viewing materials as nutrients circulating in healthy, safe metabolisms.

These were the subjects of a series of workshops. Data was collected in many ways – through activities, discussions, keeping learning diaries, completing learning activities surveys and interview forms. The details of how the workshops were organised are for another time but the findings are interesting, particularly if you keep in mind that they were in search of *perspective transformation*: in other words, they were looking to find out if their ideas about education and sustainability had been changed by the work they had done as a group.

 Read what the practitioners said and then answer these questions:

Did the activities allow them to question long-held beliefs?
Were they forced to re-assess their roles as educators?
Did they feel that working together as a group had given them more confidence?
Were they persuaded that education is the key to a sustainable future?

> *P3: When I realised that we are living in an unsustainable system, I was terrified and I was very pessimistic. We cannot continue like this. How will my child survive?*
> *P5: I wasn't aware of my negative effect on the planet. For example, I didn't know the concept of an ecological footprint.*
> *P6: Calculating our own ecological footprints resulted in important changes in my perspective. I realised that my decisions support the unsustainable situation of the planet. I looked at myself in this activity. I evaluated my actions and saw that I am doing wrong. I started being aware of the impact of my actions on the planet.*
>
> (Feriver *et al.* 2015: 730)

> *LD5: I was living in angst with the perspective that our children would be facing the prospect of a planet that would be impossible to live in. Under these circumstances, giving birth to a child does not seem rational to me.*
>
> (730)

Note: I assume that P represents participants. LD refers to Learning Diaries.

These participants appear to be shocked to have been forced to examine their own attitudes to sustainability and the last one is thinking of the future threat to her children and the children of others.

> *P6: I had the opportunity to hear things from other participants that I hadn't thought of until then. I started to learn new things from other participants which had never occurred to me before. This has motivated me to undertake further research since I did not take the statements of the other participants at face value. Only if I could corroborate their views with my research would I change my views.*
> *LD3: I noticed the positive impact of collaborative working when discussing and creating ideas with my group mates.*

P1: We started evaluating ourselves. At the end of the day, I shared everything I gained from this training with my husband. He also gave his comments.
P3: As soon as possible, I plan to meet with the parents. I will also share with my students the things that I've learned with my students.

(2015: 731)

As you can see, these participants were all reviewing the impact of being able to study or work with others.

 Now read this last extract with attention. It is concerned with aspects of consumerism, business, capitalism, greed and lack of awareness of the realities of millions in this world.

The Chair and Apple Tree activities were identified by the participants as the most significant aspects of the training that helped them at this stage. In these activities, the participants discussed production patterns of simple materials used in daily life. Their comments showed they realised that prevailing production patterns and priorities were unsustainable and that both producers and consumers have a responsibility for challenging this outcome. The training session also compared cradle-to-grave with a cradle-to-cradle approach. Participants responded to this recognising that, for example, nature itself offers a very unique model for 'production cycles' and hence for sustainable living, for example through biomimicry. Also, they understood that all stages of production can be designed according to cradle-to-cradle principles:
P6: While doing the life of an apple tree activity I asked myself the following questions: 'why don't we observe nature?' and 'how could we be so blind?' I realised that natural systems were very well designed and balanced. Our real intention should be maintaining such balance. Even though I was raised in a village, in the countryside – not being aware of these facts I mentioned hurt me a lot.
P3: Later, with the perception I gained through this training and my own parallel research, I became aware of the existence of new options and possibilities. I thought that we can move on in a more optimistic and hopeful way. I have positive feelings at the end of the training.

(732)

Not gloom and doom but a viable future

Two of the key thinkers in the world of early childhood education and care are Ingrid Pramling Samuelsson and Lilian Katz, both of whom have been and continue to be powerful advocates for education for sustainability. In their report to a conference in Gothenburg in 2004 they made some relevant points about education for sustainable development (ESD) for very young children as being certainly not about gloom and doom. Here are some of their key points:

• Children need to feel that they are a truly valued part of the community – not invisible, marginal or worthless. In other words they should be viewed as legitimate actors in shaping their communities now and in the future. This means that each child's meaning and perspective need to be heard and considered in education.

- ESD must begin in the local realities of the children's lives. This means that the starting point of any project should relate to the things that children encounter in their daily lives and can make sense of. This can broaden out to issues in the community and perhaps even to the town or city. Children are concerned about what they hear and see, which is why real-life questions have to be central for the topic of sustainable development (SD).
- Similarly, hands-on experience is important in the early years so that young children can experiment, make and try things out, consider the effects of their experiments and decide what to do next.
- ECE for SD should be locally relevant and culturally appropriate, and should reflect the seriousness of working for sustainability. So rather than merely offering recycling projects practitioners should take the questions and/or interests of the children as the starting point.
- Diversity is a feature of daily life and showing respect for others and their languages and ways of life is important. There is much to bond diverse communities when they are dealing with a serious and complex issue. And the issues involved in sustainability are both serious and complex. Children can learn about different lifestyles, and particularly about the gap between the rich and the poor.
- It is important that ECE is intellectually challenging in the sense that it is about more than learning to read and write or save water and reuse paper. In fact, Pramling Samuelsson and Katz suggest that the guiding principle should be based on the 7Rs – reduce, reuse, recycle, respect, repair, reflect and refuse (based on Pramling Samuelsson & Katz 2008: 7).

Learning from the wisdom of elders

There is much we can learn about how to protect and save our planet from those who live in much closer touch with the earth, with nature and with an ethics of care rather than consumption. Jenny Ritchie, who is based in New Zealand and has specialised in cultural, environmental and social justice, has written a chapter in *Research in Early Childhood Education for Sustainability* (Davis & Elliott 2014) on this topic.

She talks of how, along with globalisation and the flight from the countryside to cities and urban living, there is a sense that today's young children have little contact with natural wild places. I remember growing up in a city in Africa, yet managing to ramble in a park close to where we lived and where we went to look for cave paintings and stone implements. We took our holidays in one of the great game parks where elephant and lion, giraffe and zebra roamed and I fell in love with all that was wild and untamed. I certainly had a kinship with the wild and untamed but have never managed to be moved by nature in England. It seems so tame and safe. Wally Penetito (2009), a scholar of education, said that *place-based education* still plays a role in Maori education and he believes that it is essential for indigenous peoples, who still see themselves as 'co-habitors' with the environment and in the environment. Many indigenous people still see themselves as the guardians of nature.

Durie, also a Maori scholar, wrote

> *Relationships between people and the natural environments, between tangible and intangible dimensions, between organic and inorganic material, and between past and future constitute the*

foundations upon which indigenous populations understand the world. An energy flow that spirals outwards connects the multiple threads so that even very small objects become part of a wider context that gives them shape and meaning.

(2010: 239)

All of this is made apparent through stories and songs, food-gathering and healing: all aspects of life and describing and explaining life reflect a deep respect for and intimate connection with the mountains and the seas, the animals and birds, the flowers and trees. It is all summed up by the Maori saying '*Unity comes with a fair sharing of resources*' (Halba & McCallum 2011: 69).

Case Study 13: Nurturing the soul

At Hawera Kindergarten on North Island the little pot plants the children had planted had finished growing, so:

> we recycled them by transplanting succulents in the pots. First we had karakia (spiritual incantation) to acknowledge Tane Mahuta, then broke off pieces of the succulents plants, sat them in the pots and watered them. The children carried river stones from the gravel pit and poured them into the planter boxes. We talked about gardening, looking after plants, where the stones came from and experienced the mauri (life force) in the plants and stones. It was a good team effort. When we had finished the children admired their work. When one works with Papatuaniki one can find it relaxing and peaceful. It teaches patience and nurtures the soul.

(Ritchie 2014: 56)

Note: Ranginui and Papatūānuku are the primordial parents, the sky father and the earth mother who lie locked together in a tight embrace.
This, says Ritchie, illustrates how teachers can respectfully incorporate indigenous beliefs and values and customs in their daily programmes with young children.

Moving on . . .

In this chapter we looked at a number of issues, ranging from the meaning of ecological footprints and what we can learn from them; the power of interdisciplinary research; the wisdom of the elders and how to change perspectives through in-service training. In the next chapter we look at ethics and professionalism, considering how early childhood practitioners are regarded and the effect this has on them, on the children and their families.

Chapter 10

Professionalism

Key words and concepts: each stage of life as preparation for the next stage?; early childhood as a profession; views of early childhood practitioners; qualifications and training; the demands of the job; dominant discourses of maternalism; care for – care about – caregiving; emotion; attachment interactions; key worker; knowledge and good practice; globalisation; roles of teenagers.

A lot has already been said about pedagogy in this book but less about ethics or about how difficult it can be to be an ECEC practitioner. So let us start by looking at how we – early childhood practitioners – are perceived by our fellow educationalists.

Since the field of early childhood practitioners is made up primarily of women, as in so many other arenas, there is a tendency to think that the work that we do is insignificant, trivial and not serious. After all, we are 'only' women. The assumption made is that we are less well qualified than our fellow educators in primary schools and even less qualified than our fellow educators in secondary schools.

You wait until you're older

Michael Rosen, a colleague and friend, poet, performer and activist, gave me permission to cite the poem below. It appeared in the *Guardian* newspaper of 28 January 2018 – just as I was writing this chapter and seemed to me very apt.

> *You Wait Till You're Older – the curriculum as progress towards the workplace*
> *When you're at college*
> *they say*
> *this is just a holiday;*
> *you wait till you get out and face life*
> *and see what work is really like.*
>
> *When you're in your last years at school*
> *they say*
> *you wait till you get to college, or university*
> *you'll see what it's like to really get your head down and study something that the rest of your*
> *life depends on – there'll be no hiding place then.*

When you're doing your GCSEs
they say
you wait till you do your last two years at school
you'll see it's much harder, much more intensive,
much more to learn, much more to know, and if you fall behind, you won't get into college or
university and that's a choice you want to be able to make and not miss out on the chance just
because you weren't prepared to work hard now.

When you're doing your first years at secondary school,
they say
you wait till you're doing your GCSEs you'll
have to really get your head down and learn much more stuff than we're giving you now, this
is just a taster, but you had better get used to it, so that it won't come as so much of a shock
then.

When you're in your last years at primary school
they say
you wait till you get to secondary school
it's going to be a big, big surprise when you see
how much homework you'll have to do
so you might as well do plenty now to get in the swing of it, and remember:
the marks you get now, go with you to secondary school and will determine what GCSEs
you do, and you know: what GCSEs you do will determine whether you go to university
or not.

When you're in the first years at primary school
they say
that you have to get used to doing this
kind of work because coming up soon there's going to be plenty more work like this and it's best
to learn now how to do it, or you won't know where you are when it comes along later
and suddenly you'll find that you're left behind

When you're in nursery school,
they say
it's best to get used to sitting down for hours on end to get used to what you'll have to do when
you go to university.

When you're in playgroup,
they say
it's best to not run around all the time and get in some time sitting still and listening so that
you get a feel of school and college and life and work.

When you're in that time before playgroup
they say
that you've got to get used to the time when your parents aren't there, and you've got to do
just as you're told because one day, you'll have exams which decide what you're going to work
at for the rest of your life.

Does life have to be like this? Everything you do is in order to equip you for the next stage? Thinking of education like this is so damaging for everyone concerned – for the children and their parents, for the teachers and the carers, for management, inspectors, planners. It is essential that we revise such views. Seeing each stage of life as the preparation for the next stage is a stultifying view of the social and cultural worlds of teaching and learning. It is within a culture that largely holds this view that so many early childhood teachers and carers feel insignificant and undervalued.

As we take note of or choose to be blind to what is happening to the natural world we can also take note of or choose to be blind to what is happening to those tasked with educating the young children whose futures we are preparing for. The reality is that the work that we do is very significant. We are working with those whose futures we are holding in our hands. In terms of educating these young children for sustainability there can be no more significant task.

We know that those involved in ECEC come from a range of training backgrounds. Traditionally, where early childhood provision was split into either care or education, the two disciplines were regarded as being quite separate. To be a teacher in the UK, for example, you needed to have followed an educational programme and acquired a certificate or degree or higher qualification in education. To be a carer there were fewer requirements and much of the training was in the form of short or in-service training. In some integrated settings there are educators/carers having had different types of training, often doing slightly different jobs and often on different pay scales. In good provision there is an ethos associated with working within teams of people. How this is decided seems to be up to the country, the regulations, the age groupings of the children, the views held of young learners and pedagogy.

But there are some common and significant issues associated with being an early childhood practitioner.

 What issues can you think of that are particular to being an early childhood practitioners?

The field is dominated by women and it is notable that many of them are treated as being inferior to other teachers. The early childhood field is still embedded in the dominant discourses of maternalism. Dr Maria Montessori, that significant figure in early childhood, actually wrote these words:

> *The teacher, as part of the environment, must herself be attractive, preferably young and beautiful, charmingly dressed, scented with cleanliness, happy and graciously dignified. This is the ideal, and cannot always be perfectly reached, but the teacher who presents herself to the children should remember that they are great people, to whom she owes understanding and respect. She should study her movements, making them gentle and graceful as possible, that the child may unconsciously pay her the compliment of thinking her as beautiful as his mother, who is naturally his ideal of beauty.*
>
> (1946: 87)

Words fail me!

Early childhood practitioners are often on lower salaries for longer periods than other teachers and there are fewer possibilities of being in more senior roles, earning more money. How, we might ask, are they able to buy their beautiful clothes, prerequisites for them to look like mother substitutes?

Many are reluctant to apply for management posts or argue for better pay and conditions having been told that working with the younger children requires the least intellectual prowess.

Yet in reality their job is very demanding physically, intellectually and emotionally. Some have to deal with babies and toddlers, which is physically and emotionally draining. Others deal with preschool age children, some of whom are in settings where there is a curriculum to adhere to with some standards or tests at the end of certain stages.

Many speak of feeling lonely, drained, not respected, not consulted, not autonomous, exhausted, unable to make changes and generally not regarded as being a professional. Here is a quotation from Steedman (cited in Taggart):

> *I loved my children and worked hard for them, lay awake at night worrying about them, spent my Sundays making work-cards, recording stories for them to listen to, planning the week ahead. My back ached as I pinned their paintings to the wall, wrote the labels with a felt-tip pen, a good round hand, knowing then the irony with which I would recall in later years the beacon light of the martyr's classroom shining into the winter's evening, the cleaner's broom moving through the corridor of the deserted schoolhouse.*

(1987: 118)

More on care and ethics

It is much simpler to think and talk about education than to do so about care. I think it is because care is so multifaceted. We talk about care as an emotional response and also as labour associated with women's work in the home or in low-paid and low-status work. Historically care was seen primarily as 'what women do' and this feminisation of the profession of childcare in particular has undervalued the vital work of caring for young children and even more so caring for babies. In some eyes care is something that is essentially feminine and 'natural'. 'Proper' education is what happens in school and then university.

Davis and Degotardi (2015) state that in reality care has been seen as an integral aspect of teaching for many years, particularly in the case of young children. Care has also been seen as an essential disposition by parents and by teachers during teaching practice. Aspiring early childhood practitioners are expected to adopt what might be called an ethical or moral approach to practice in the sense of caring for the self, others, ideas and the natural world.

 What acts can you think of that practitioners engage in regularly that might be described as caring?

Babies and toddlers need not only physical care like having their nappies changed, being put down to sleep, drinking their milk or juice, but also care in the sense of knowing that they are cared about as well as cared for. Caregiving is the emotional and subtle art of knowing each child and her needs and desires and being able to address them. Those working with young children also need to care not only about the children but also about the natural world. One of the key roles of early childhood educators is to model respect, care and appreciation for one another and for the world we live in. More than that they need to find ways to enable children to care for and about one another and for the world they live in. Part of the role of those working with babies and toddlers is to encourage them to do things for themselves – to become more independent. Fisher and Tronto (1990) say that the word *caregiver* signifies more than taking care of. According to them it is done daily, is hands-on and involves decision-making and intense time commitments.

 Read the comment below from Tinny, an ECEC practitioner cited in Davis and Degotardi (2015), as she reflects on some of the challenges her job offers and decide if she has a case.

I think for care with the age group I work with, I feel like it is . . . a lot of people have the impression that it's just about caring because they're under two's, you can't really educate them or teach them anything but, I think care also goes into that whole aspect and notion of having a relationship that is more than just surface, it's about knowing the ins and outs of each other so, I think it would be good if it was used more in the EYLF and how it would be able to relate to this age group.

(2015: 1742)

Note: The EYLF is the Australian Early Years Learning Framework.

The impact of the complexity of attachment interactions in early childhood settings

Jools Page and Peter Elfer (2013), two researchers in the UK, carried out a case study of just one nursery using in-depth interviews, group discussions and daily diaries for the staff exploring how their interactions with their small 'clients' could be warm, responsive and highly individual, but also how vulnerable these interactions were, being susceptible to being disrupted or disturbed. In short they were looking at what practitioners knew and understood about attachments. You will almost certainly have heard of John Bowlby who first examined and wrote about the significance of an infant being able to bond with a consistent parent figure as a safe base from which to explore and form relationships with others. He called this an attachment and his work became known as *attachment theory*. For an infant or young child, starting in an early childhood setting means leaving the safety of the home and parents for a new place, unknown faces and different ways of being. It is an intensely emotional time for the children and for their parents and, of course, for the practitioners. Having a '*replacement parent*' can be good but there are complications as, for example, where the mother of a child begins to feel that she has been replaced and the key worker feels guilty for being seen as a mother substitute. In the literature on the subject much has been said about how difficult it is for a practitioner who, herself, does not feel cared for to be able to care for others. Early childhood practitioners require emotional resilience.

Page and Elfer also explored the views of staff about their work being almost entirely intuitive with little or no theoretical basis and not much offered in-service training.

This perceived gap in the training of early childhood practitioners is surprising because much has been written about how able very young children are at forming attachments. In many settings children are given a '*key worker*' who becomes the primary person to monitor and relate to the child. It is a time-consuming, delicate, emotionally draining and expensive model, but one that is much needed in the settings of early childhood and many practitioners think it should operate not only with babies and toddlers but also with older children. The nursery (which was in effect a children's centre) where the research took place had places for 100 children (from birth to 3 years old) and was set in an urban English region. The staff–child ratio was the national one, which is 1 adult per 3 children aged 0–2, 1 adult per 4 children aged 2–3 years. The staff included senior staff with graduate teacher qualifications; some staff holding vocational qualifications, and some still studying.

 I am going to cite some of the things said by members of staff and parents and, remember, as you read them, try to tell how easy or difficult, simple or complicated, calm or emotional, valued or not the practitioners feel.

- Fatima said, '*Dae Ho he'd come from Korea, parents were studying and stuff and he cried for eight weeks constantly*' (Page & Elfer 2013: 559).
- Suzy said, '*The key person is responsible for doing all the nappy changes . . . it's quite a special time, you don't wanting anybody changing your nappy, I mean it can be quite frightening. . . . We try to spend meal times with your family group, that's hard because staff have got to go off and have their lunch*' (559).
- Fatima said, '*I don't think I have been supported that much by . . . I ended up going to see him and saying . . . how do you cope with children that have been constantly crying week after week . . . nobody's come to offer help to us*' (561).

A beat of life again. . .

The work that early childhood practitioners do is so intense and emotional and sometimes tragic and at other times wondrous that it is at the same time rewarding and exhausting. It involves working with children who are sometimes too young to be able to clearly communicate their needs and desires, who express their frustration without restraint, who are in a new and strange environment at first and are having to make new relationships. So early childhood practitioners have to have immense patience and also an intense interest in what the children are paying attention to. Trainees are rarely taught how to really listen to young children on their initial training programmes and it is primarily through this listening that they become able to enter the fascinating worlds of making sense of the world in all its complexity. A pedagogy of listening allows practitioners like Vea Vecchi in Reggio Emilia to notice the fine details of what children say and do and then be able to understand what it is the child is taking notice of.

The realities of the work that early childhood practitioners do

Vea Vecchi has spent her professional life not only watching and hearing young children but also watching and hearing her colleagues. She is perceptive, aware, attuned and critical of some of the things she has observed in her career. One of the questions she asks is why some people think that working with young children is simple. She says that

very often, only physical fatigue associated with the work is taken into consideration, not all the mental juggling that must be done to have their attention, interest, concentration, trust and friendship. But when you manage to have their friendship, then children are courageous, you can propose difficult projects and they will stand by you in trying them out, get enthusiastic, get their parents involved, be willing to stay on longer at school. When children are motivated, they like doing difficult things.

She cites the touching story of Leonardo who got anxious whenever asked to do anything and ended up asking to '*go pee pee*' but at the end of a long day would state '*There! We've done a really good job today*' (2010: 150).

Qualifications, education and professional development matter

The OECD produces regular reports on many aspects of early childhood education under the heading of *Encouraging Quality in Early Childhood Education and Care* (ECEC) and you can find them online if you are interested. I propose to look closely at the one that is the research brief asking if the evidence shows that changes to qualifications, education and professional development matter.

Let's start by classifying the terms.

- ECEC qualifications indicate the recognised level and type of knowledge, skills and competencies that staff have received.
- Formal education in ECEC refers to the levels and type of education that staff pursue to acquire the knowledge, skills and competencies to work in the sector.
- Professional development is what staff already working in the sector may be offered in order to improve or update their practice. This is also called in-service training, continuous education or professional training.

In an ever changing world recent social and cultural changes have challenged the accepted or traditional views of childhood and of child-rearing. This includes the fact that women now play a much more active role in the world of work; poverty, war and globalisation have ensured we have more ethnic diversity in our settings; and there are greatly changing views on the purpose of early education. I imagine you can work out the impact this has on government planning to fund improving levels and quality of educating staff. OECD accepts that having highly educated and appropriately paid staff is the key factor in raising quality.

The report makes a very important point in saying that it is not necessarily the qualifications of the staff alone that have an effect on the quality of early childhood settings but *what* knowledge the staff have about young children and their needs, how they view young children as communicators and thinkers, their abilities to plan, observe, record, interact with and relate to the children. There is evidence that shows that the more qualified the staff are the higher the quality, but the issue is very complex. So perhaps it is what the staff have studied, what they value, and how they apply this to working with young children that is more important. In other words we are looking at what is essential for practitioners to know. Based on the work of Sheridan and Pramling Samuelsson, it is believed that the skills and traits that will positively impact on the learning and development of young children are as follows:

- Have a good understanding of how children develop and learn.
- Know each child as an individual with a past and a present and a future.

- View children, from birth, as competent, communicative and intent on becoming members of their culture and community.
- Take children seriously.
- Be able to listen to and observe young children in order to use what they say or reveal as a starting point for more exploration.
- Be able to develop children's perspectives.
- Be able to praise, comfort, question, answer, support and be responsive to the children.
- Be attentive to children's feelings, fears, needs, desires, interests and moods.
- Understand and be able to create and work in enriched environments where there are opportunities and materials to stimulate children's interests.
- Come to know what interests, concerns or stimulates each child.
- Willingness to know something about and show respect for each child's culture, language, family structure and ethnicity.
- Be organised and able to plan, record what is seen and heard, keep records.
- Establish positive relationships with family members.
- Value being part of the team of practitioners in the ECEC setting.

This is a detailed list and an indication of just how demanding the roles of early childhood practitioners are. It seems evident to me that if you are working with children everything you do is related to caring for and about them and if you are paying attention to what they say and do and respond appropriately you are involved in their learning. For me care and education are inextricably linked.

 What does all of this have to do with educating young children for a sustainable shared world?

The children who are now in our early childhood settings are the one who are most likely to have to live with what we have done and still continue to do to the world. If we educate them now to know what we need to change about our values, behaviour, practices, attitudes there may be hope. We need then to encourage them to be able to critique our actions and explain why. We have to educate them as thinking, questioning, thoughtful and creative people who, if they can learn to collaborate and work with others, try to use their combined brain power and ingenuity to come up with solutions. So the early childhood practitioners of today need to be regarded, respected and rewarded as highly skilled thinkers, capable of influencing a generation to come. We need to listen to their ideas, respond to their suggestions, equip them to make whatever they need.

Sustainable leadership in the early years

Jan Georgeson, in Huggins and Evans (2018), is one of the few to consider the role of sustainable leadership in early childhood settings. There is some debate about exactly what the role of the leader is. Some argue that it is limited to managing resources, leading the curriculum and sustaining those working in the setting. Others argue that it is also about establishing and maintaining community links. Let us examine some of these in more detail and with particular reference to sustainability.

Managing resources

This is a task to terrify even the most intrepid leaders. Whatever decisions you make will inevitably offend someone on the staff. If you mention spending money on new books for the nursery someone will almost certainly claim that there are enough books and we need another member of staff. And adding sustainability to the list of urgent needs really does sound beyond possibility. Georgeson suggests a good place to start is with an audit – conducted best by someone other than you – to establish a baseline for your use of resources. By resources, are we talking of electricity, water and gas and also paper towels and tissues and toilet roll? What learning chemicals do you use? And how much recycling do you do and if so, how much? Knowing the facts you lead your team in discussion of what you all think you needs to change, what to keep and what to discard. We know that early years practice has a long and honourable track record of recycling, coping with reusable sustainable materials. When I first worked in the UK in an early years setting I was horrified to find staff using food stuffs like dry pasta or rice or lentils as materials for collage. I swiftly banned the practice and then had to face the wrath of the middle-class parents insisting that such tactile materials were ideal for exploration. In South Africa no one would ever stick anything edible on anything other than the tongue! Food is for eating and not for playing with.

But – there is always a but – we need to try to avoid giving out confusing messages. Here is the advice offered by NAAEE: '*it is important to recognise differences in families regarding attitudes toward their children's handling of certain insects or creatures and their reverence toward some animals or plants in nature. Corn or maize is revered in traditional Mexican culture*' (2010: 13).

Sustaining people

This is the most important role of a staff leader – to manage human resources so that they do not deplete their store of goodwill. Demanding too much of people can only be damaging. So, as leader it is important to get to know what the specific skills, talents, interests, abilities, likes and dislikes are, as well as knowing what – if anything – scares them.

> *Becoming critically reflexive about our own and other's emotional reactions allows us to step away from the immediacy of the reaction and work towards more constructive responses in the future . . .. The embodied wisdom developed through being reflexive about emotions allows for empathy felt towards others to be guided by deep insight into the societal conditions, such as gender, which shape and constrain them. Assisting educators, for example, to view the tensions that frequently occur between colleagues as the consequence of the increasing pressures of the workplace and the lack of funding or support, is far more helpful than allowing them to feel this as a personal failure. It invites a fundamentally different response, centred around collective political action rather than personally giving up early childhood work . . .. The societal reluctance to value early childhood work highly is an attempt to keep in place systems of power which have seen women and the less economically privileged made responsible for the care and emotional well-being of others, whether in the paid work of nursing, eldercare or childcare, or the unpaid work of mothering.. . . Burnout and staff turnover are responses, I suggest, to the intractability of a system that values early childhood work so poorly. Developing more thoughtful emotional*

responses to the stresses of the work builds a more resilient workforce, but also, importantly, one with the emotional insight to be able to challenge the inequities of the system, knowing that these are not simply individual problems.

(Yarrow 2015: 361)

Moving on . . .

In this chapter we have turned our attention to aspects of qualifications, professionalism, self-esteem, knowledge, good practice, being a leader – all mostly issues related to the adults working in the early childhood sector and responsible for including sustainability in an already overworked and underfunded sector. In the next and last chapter we look for glimmers of hope . . .

Chapter 11

Building hope

Sustainability is such a vast subject that no one book can even start to do it justice. In this, the last chapter in the book, I propose offering some projects and thoughts from across the world to illustrate how brilliant young children are and how dedicated to their futures their parents and carers and educators are. I hope the selection makes you not only smile but also hope.

The *Silkworm Project* in Japan

You will almost certainly know that the kimono was the traditional dress in Japan and that the kimonos were made of silk. Today almost all the kimono industries have gone and so have the silkworms and the wonderful fields of mulberry trees on which the silkworms fed. When I was a little girl in South Africa we had a mulberry tree in our garden and my dad – who loved teasing – told me that, if the silkworms I kept in a shoe box with holes in the lid were given mulberry leaves to eat, the silk they spun would be pink and if they were given cabbage leaves the silk they spun would be white. I thought it strange that my silkworms all produced the same coloured silk whatever I fed them.

Osama Fujii, who is the director of Takatsukasa Hoikuen Childcare Centre in Nishijin – a quarter where there had been groves of mulberry trees in the past – set up a special environmental project known as the *Silkworm Project*. It carried on for 4 years and involved not only the children in the centre but also local farmers and community members. The garden of the centre became a place for environmental learning and offered hands-on experience for the children as they attempted to discover answers to their questions. If you have kept silkworms yourself you will know what a perfect example they are of the transformative life-cycle of a living creature and one that lasts for only about 25 days. The silkworms are easy to look after and simple for small hands to hold. Children can be helped to remove the silk and then make the cocoon into a finger doll, which is dyed or painted. The children can also watch the making of the cocoon and observe the worms moving using a magnifying glass.

What is also relevant is that the project was not only about the natural world but also about culture and economy when the teachers talked to the children about the beginnings and history of silk clothing and the silk industry.

(based on Fujii & Izumi, in Pramling Samuelsson and Kaga, 2008: 87–93)

The earthworms project in Brazil

In the same book edited by Pramling Samuelsson and Kaga (2008) there is the description of another worm project, this time from Brazil. Vital Didonet tells the reader that the Earthworm project originated not through the ideas of an adult but through the discovery by little Felipe of an earthworm in the dry leaves under an orange tree in the garden of his early childhood centre. He called his friends, one of whom knew it was an earthworm. The children played with it, trying to put it on a leaf, turning it over with a stick and putting soil beside it. On their return to the classroom the children kept talking about it until Luisa said 'My father creates earthworms. The teacher, unsure of what this meant asked again and this time Luisa said 'He sells earthworm manure.' The discussion carried on as the teacher got the children to offer their ideas about why earthworms make manure and what manure is used for. Out of that grew the project. The children started to find out about the tunnels made by earthworms, what they ate and why they hate sunlight. They invited Luisa's father in to talk about his work and decided they would build an earthworm house. Luisa's dad brought in an earthworm house made of glass so the children could watch the worms and talked to the children about how they multiply, create humus and what humus does to help plants.

The children used the Internet and, helped by the teacher, they decided to collect the materials they thought they would need to make the earthworm house. The choice of the materials was a complex one and involved the children in making decisions and justifying them. So, (for example) someone brought aluminium foil to make it dark so that the worms were not exposed to light; they gathered food leftovers for the worms to feed on and filled their construction with soil, sand and dry leaves and covered it in black plastic. They peered through the gaps in plastic to observe every day and when the plastic was fully removed after four weeks the layers were all mixed. One of the children brilliantly called the earthworms 'soil workers'.

When the project ended the children were inspired to cultivate a vegetable garden at the school and make a flowerbed for medicinal plants (based on Didonet, in Pramling Samuelsson and Kaga, 2008: 28–29).

'No society that loved children would consign nearly one in five to poverty' (David Orr 2001)

No society that loved its children would put them in front of television for 4 hours each day. No society that loved its children would lace their food, air, water, and soil with thousands of chemicals whose total effect cannot be known. No society that loved its children would build so many prisons and so few parks and schools. No society that loved its children would teach them to recognize over 1000 corporate logos but fewer than a dozen plants and animals native to their home places. No society that loved its children would divorce them so completely from contact with soils, forests, streams, and wildlife. No society that loved its children would create places like the typical suburb or shopping mall. No society that loved its children would casually destroy real neighborhoods and communities in order to build even more highways. No society that loved its children would build so many glitzy sports stadiums while its public schools fall apart. No society that loved its children would build more shopping malls than high schools (Suzuki, 23). No society that loved its children would pave over 1,000,000 acres each year for even more shopping malls and parking lots. No society that loved its children would knowingly run even a small risk of future climatic disaster. No society that loved its children would use the practice of discounting in order to ignore its future problems. No society that loved its children would leave behind a legacy of ugliness and biotic impoverishment.

(http://designshare.com/research/orr/loving_children.htm)

Note: David Orr was professor and chair of the Environmental Studies Programme at Oberlin College and wrote this in 2001. The piece is called 'Loving Children: A Design Problem'. I have retained the American spellings.

The case studies and examples that follow all come from the UNESCO report entitled 'Education for Sustainable Development: Good Practices in Early Childhood'. Education for Sustainable Development in Action: Good Practice No. 4 (2012).

The *Sucateca* in the Eco-Patrulha project at Oga Mita School, Portugal

Oga Mitá means the 'House of the Child' and is a preschool in the town of Porto. It was one of the facilities named by UNESCO as offering good practice in education for sustainable development in early childhood in 2012. The project arose out of children raising issues about what they saw as environmentally appropriate behaviour that should be kept and what was environmentally inappropriate behaviour to be changed. They made a list for each of these and displayed the lists on the doors so that teachers and parents and carers and visitors might see them. From these lists they made plans covering a number of school years. They made an Eco-Patrulha, which means an eco-patro logo, to label things with. They started to make collections of all sorts of things – of plastic bottle tops, used batteries and food oils – and eventually set up a space for the storage of everyday waste. This was the *Sucateca* (which literally means 'succeeds'), which was a space where they could all meet to organise the reuse of discarded materials like newspapers, magazines, the packing material of hygiene products or food, damaged CDs, cardboard boxes, buttons, scraps of tissue and more. The aim was to recycle these in the creative expression of their feelings through collage or sculpture or other artworks. You may remember that 'reuse' is one of the 7R words cited earlier in the book. They set up a biological kitchen garden using organic compound to prepare the soil for growing crops to be used for school meals and they composed a hymn, which ends with the refrain

All the waste we make
We must be a-sorting;
We take it to the eco-point
And it goes for re-cycling (UNESCO 2012: 33–37).

Leuchtpol – energy and the environment: a preschool project in Germany

Leuchtpol is a non-profit organisation for promoting environmental education at preschool level and has its head office in Frankfurt, Germany. Also included in the UNESCO review of early childhood education, the project is not one about the children themselves but refers to a 5-day training programme for early childhood practitioners designed by Leuchtpol as a follow up to an original workshop on energy and the environment. Leuchtpol had noticed that energy was rarely talked of or developed in early childhood settings so here we find an unusual alliance between an environmental organisation which is a NGO and an energy group. This is what their brochure on the Internet says about their organisation:

> *Leuchtpol supports education for sustainable development via the examples of energy and the environment at kindergartens. The main focus of the further training courses, which also include the latest findings in education at pre-school/ kindergarten level, is always on the children's skills. The Frankfurt headquarters and the regional offices are implementing the project through further training, consultation and support, and materials. At the Leuchtpol further training courses, educators gain the basic knowledge they need to apply this subject area in the everyday life at the kindergarten. The children are encouraged to explore, question and discuss all forms of energy in their everyday lives. They are able to recognise that every action, such as converting one form of energy to another, brings about changes and has consequences.*
> (http://www.leuchtpol.de/eng/further-information/infoflyer-english.pdf)

Leuchtpol has strong links to ANU, which is the umbrella organisation of environmental education in Germany. UNESCO said that they considered this venture as good practice because Leuchtpol offers '*a potential blueprint*' for ESD which might allow further projects to be developed with the involvement of parents and a consideration of intercultural backgrounds (UNESCO 2012: 27–32).

Childhood health, care and development where there is or was no school system

After the model of advanced and wealthy Germany we turn to 'The Sustainable Human Development Project' in Ecuador and Peru where, amazingly, we find another example of good practice identified by UNESCO 2012. The aims of this project are tragically small:

(1)   the right to a good start in life;
(2)   the right to a name and a nationality;
(3)   the right to health;
(4)   the right to quality basic education (UNESCO 2012: 48).

One of the features of this programme, which accounts for its success, is the respect and attention given to intercultural strategies. Most notable relates to birth practices, where recognition has been given to the custom for the whole family to be present for the birth and it is all family members who care for the woman in labour. Women give birth squatting and go, afterwards, to the San Jose de Morona where they can see a doctor. There is no ethnical discrimination.

The project also set up mobile brigades to register births or dealt with the late registration of births in remote regions. This is an attempt to ensure that every Ecuadorian child can have an identity card.

And the project also developed a community-based family and children facility for those in the Amazonian region (UNESCO 2012: 48–50).

Raglan Road Community Centre: hope exemplified

I was so delighted to find a South African early childhood setting cited as a model of good practice in terms of ECECfSD that I saved it for last! It was a community centre in Grahamstown in the Cape Province and the children came from every type of deprivation you can imagine. It was and probably still is a community where unemployment is the norm. Alcoholism was rampant as was ill health, hunger and malnutrition. Child abuse was common and it is not surprising that such dire poverty was accompanied by poor levels of health and education. The way in which the staff decided to tackle the multiple and complex problems was through multi-pronged programmes aimed at empowering the young children through developing their skills and education using whatever was available in terms of resources and providing activities suitable for the preschoolers and the primary and secondary care-givers. This is South Africa where one child caring for another is common practice. The staff recognised early on that in order to succeed in their aims they had to adopt a truly community-involvement approach so that everyone became a learner and everyone became a 'teacher'. In such a community what mattered most were these essentials: food, safety, health, ways of expressing feelings, generating income, understanding the hazards of alcohol and child abuse, an awareness of human rights and sustainability. That is an extraordinary list of essentials.

In this community centre the partners or stakeholders included: the government at district/province and state level; local authorities; preschool institutions; research institutions and community organisations. The groups of learners were multiple. There were young children aged from 3 to 7 years, community members who were involved as crafters, community members involved as herbalists and clinic staff and community members who were largely illiterate or semiliterate. And, of course, the school teachers. A great deal of thought was involved in designing the programme. Any idea was first piloted and then implemented slowly according to how the community responded. The project was underpinned by a sound understanding of how young children learn best, always taking into account the particular needs, interests and concerns of the children. There was a strong focus on creating stronger social networks. Both English and Xhosa, the home language of the community, were used. Some details of the programme are listed here.

- All learning tasks were aimed at developing practical skills, knowledge and resilience building and based on the philosophy that young active learners need to learn to think and express ideas, make things and share them, assess what they were doing and what effect it had on them and their peers and on their environment.
- In order to deal with hunger, meals were provided as part of the school day and, to make sure what was on offer was healthy, a food garden was established in the grounds and then became a learning resource for the children and in addition offered a resource income for those in the community who worked in the garden and got some of the produce as 'salary'.
- To tackle health issues, the centre attempted to make links with the local government clinic – but sadly the clinic itself was under-resourced. The project decided to turn to indigenous ways of dealing with illness. Elderly members of the community were asked to offer their skills both to grow the plants needed and make them into traditional medicines. A herbal garden was started and one of the teachers was training in order to facilitate the sharing of knowledge.

- To help the younger children – the primary children – it was decided to start a project on crafts so that things could be made to generate income.
- There were classes in maths, computer and literacy for the adults so that they could help the young children learn to read and write and add and also to improve their own skills.
- There were classes on social and health issues for adults and children on alcoholism and child abuse and there was a great emphasis on the rights of the children. The young children became the advocates for their rights and were said to be the most vocal advocates of their own rights (UNESCO 2012: 7–12).

But sadly . . .

Although the centre still exists, it seems that it no longer operates as an early childhood facility. The last thing I could find out about it was that the buildings were used during the Fingo Festival in the town and, if you are interested, you can find out more online by going to YouTube at https://www.youtube.com/watch?v=eCB1KwAC1dM.

UNESCO's evaluation remains, however, to summarise just what the project achieved:

> The centre has successfully integrated social development projects into a framework that meets the needs of early childhood learners in an environmentally sustainable manner. Not only do the projects provide needful skills to adults within the community, but these skills are focused on creating sustainable socio-environmental safety nets for the children attending the ECD programme that is at the heart of the centre.

(2012: 12)

What children say

In a project to discover what young children in Sweden understood about one of the deeper issues involved in sustainability, namely economic inequality, Farhana Borg (2017) studied the responses of 53 preschool children and used the work of Bruner showing that young children learn best through having access to pictures (or icons). The children were given coloured pictures of a toy shop and of a child playing with toys, together with a puppet, which asked the children three questions:

(1) Can all children in the world afford to buy toys from a shop?
(2) Why do you think that all children (can or cannot) afford to buy toys from a shop?
(3) From where have you got to know this?

It looks like a rather clumsy approach but the answers are revealing.

- Child 5 said: '*some people don't have money, but some people have a lot of money. Some people can be very rich. The King is rich*' (6).
- Child 40 said: '*some countries are poor and children in those countries must work. Their mum and dad don't have much money*' (6).
- Child 32 said: '*all children in the world cannot afford to buy toys from a shop because their parents cannot earn that much money. They have not studied in a good school They are poor*' (6).

- Child 25 said: '*children in Africa do not have much money. They are poor*' (9).
- Child 43 said: '*There are people who often come to Sweden and sit besides shops; they are poor. They come here and there are more and more of them. Some of them do not have any money in the beginning*' (11).

From the responses of only five children we get a sense of just how thoughtful and aware young children are about abstract ideas like the inequalities in a society where most people are poor but some, like the King, are rich: that in order to have money people have to work; that poverty comes about through poor education; that everyone in Africa is poor and that refugees come because they have no money and then have to beg for it.

Bibliography

Aadnegard, S. & Kolbeinsdottir, G. (2008). The prawn stench (Appendix to Norddahl). In I. Pramling Samuelsson and Y. Kaga (eds), *The contribution of early childhood education to a sustainable society*. Paris: UNESCO. p. 78.

Agut, P.M., Angeles, U.M., & Pilar, A.M. (2014). Education for sustainable development in early childhood education in Spain. Evolution, trends and proposals. *European Early Childhood Education Research Journal*, 22(2): 213–228.

Alvestad, M. & Pramling Samuelsson, I. (1999). A comparison of the National Preschool Curricula in Norway and Sweden. *Early Childhood Research and Practice*, 1(2).

Ärlemalm-Hagsér, E. (2013). Minds on Earth Hour – a theme for sustainability in Swedish early childhood education. *Early Child Development and Care*, 183(12): 1782–1795.

Bell, D., Jean-Sigur, R.E., & Kim, Y.A. (2015). Going global in early childhood education. *Childhood Education*, 91(2): 90–100.

Bocoum, H. (2016). *Global report on culture for sustainability*. Paris: UNESCO.

Borg, F. (2017). Economic (in)equality and sustainability: Preschool children's views of the economic situation of other children in the world. *Early Child Development and Care*. https://doi.org/10.1080/03004430.2017.1372758

BRIC Project. (2017). Guidelines on community engagement: Young children, public spaces and democracy. Intellectual output 07. www.bricproject.org/wpcontent/uploads/2017/10/BRIC_guidelines_FINAL.pdf

Brock, A. (2009). *Dimensions of early years professionalism – attitudes versus competences?* or *Seven dimensions of professionalism for early years education and care: a model of professionalism for interdisciplinary practice?* (Paper presented at the British Educational Research Association Annual Conference, University of Manchester, 2–5 September 2009.)

Bronfenbrenner, U. (1979). *The ecology of human development*. Cambridge, MA: Harvard University Press.

Brundtland Commission. (1987). *Our common future*, also known as the *Brundtland Report*, from the United Nations World Commission on Environment and Development (WCED). Oxford: Oxford University Press.

Bruner, J.S. (1996). *The culture of education*. Cambridge, MA: Harvard University Press.

Burbules, N.C. (1995). *From the Editor*. Department of Educational Policy Studies University of Illinois at Urbana-Champaign.

Chan, M. (2013) Linking child survival and child development for health, equity, and sustainable development. *The Lancet*, 381(9877): 1514–1515.

Children aged five and six from the Fiastri and Rodari Municipal Schools of Sant'Ilario D'enzo (2001). *The future is a lovely day*. Reggio Children.

Cohen, E.F. (2005). Neither seen nor heard: Children's citizenship in contemporary democracies. *Citizenship Studies*, 9(2): 221–240.

Cribb, A. & Ball, S.J. (2005). Towards an ethical audit of the privatisation of education. *British Journal of Educational Studies*, 53(2): 115–128.

Cutter-Mackenzie, A. (2009). Multicultural school gardens: Creating engaging garden spaces in learning about language, culture and environment. *Canadian Journal of Environmental Education*, 14(1): 122–135.

Dahlberg, G. & Moss, P. (2005). *Ethics and politics in early childhood education*. London: RoutledgeFalmer.

Dahlberg, G. & Moss, P. (2007). Beyond quality in early childhood education and care – Languages of evaluation. *CESifo DICE Report*, 6(2): 21–26. doi:10.4324/9780203966150

Dahlberg, G., Moss, P., & Pence, A. (1999). *Beyond quality in early childhood education and care: Postmodern perspectives*. London: Falmer Press.

Davis, B. & Degotardi, S. (2015). Who cares? Infant educators' responses to professional discourses of care. *Early Child Development and Care*, 185(11/12), 1733–1747.

Davis, J. & Elliott, S. (eds). (2014). *Research in early childhood education for sustainability: International perspectives and provocations*. London and New York: Routledge.

Davis, J.M. (2005). Educating for sustainability in the early years: Creating cultural change in a child care setting. *Australian Journal of Environmental Education*, 21: 47–55.

Davis, J.M. (2008). What might education for sustainability look like in early childhood? A case for participatory, whole-of-settings approaches. In I. Pramling Samuelson and Y. Kaga (eds), *The contribution of early childhood education to a sustainable society*. Paris: UNESCO, pp. 18–24.

DiCarlo, C.F., Baumgartner, J., Ota, C., & Jenkins, C. (2015). Preschool teachers' perceptions of rough and tumble play vs aggression in preschool-aged boys. *Early Childhood Development and Care*, 185: 779–790.

Didonet, V. (2008). Early childhood education for a sustainable society. In I. Pramling Samuelson and Y. Kaga (eds), *The contribution of early childhood education to a sustainable society*. Paris: UNESCO, pp. 25–30.

Durie, E.T. (2010). Treaty claims and self determination, ManuAo lecture series, 3 March 2010.

Dyment, J.E., Davis, J.M., Nailon, D., Emery, S., Getenet, S., McCrea, N., & Hill, A. (2014). The impact of professional development on early childhood educators' confidence, understanding and knowledge of education for sustainability. *Environmental Education Research*, 20(5): 660–679.

Dýrfjörð, K. & Magnúsdóttir, B.R. (2016). Privatization of early childhood education in Iceland, *Research in Comparative & International Education*, 11(1): 80–97.

Edwards, S., Skouteris, H., Rutherford, L., & Cutter-Mackenzie, A. (2013). 'It's all about Ben10™': Children's play, health and sustainability decisions in the early years. *Early Child Development and Care*, 183(2): 280–293.

Elfer, P. & Page, J. (2015). *Pedagogy with babies: Perspectives of eight nursery managers. Early Child Development and Care*, 185: 11–12.

Engdahl, I. (2015). Early childhood education for sustainability: The OMEP World Project. *International Journal of Early Childhood*, 47(3): 347–366.

Engdahl, I. & Ärlemalm-Hagsér, E. (2008). Swedish preschool children show interest and are involved in the future of the world – Children's voices must influence education for sustainable development. In I. Pramling Samuelsson and Y. Kaga (eds), *The contribution of early childhood education to a sustainable society*. Paris: UNESCO, pp. 116–121.

Engle, P.L., Fernald, L.C., Alderman, H., Behrman, J., O'Gara, C., Yousafzai, A., de Mello, M.C, Hidrobo, M., Ulkuer, N., Ertem, I., Iltus, S. and the Global Child Development Steering Group. (2011). Strategies for reducing inequalities and improving developmental outcomes for young children in low-income and middle-income countries. *The Lancet*, 378(9799), 1339–1353.

Erikson, K.G. (2013). Why education for sustainable development needs early childhood education: The case of Norway. *Journal of Teacher Education for Sustainability*, 15: 120.

Esposito, J. & Swain, A. (2009). Pathways to social justice: Urban teachers' uses of culturally relevant pedagogy as a conduit for teaching for social justice. *Perspectives on Urban Education*, 6(1): 38–48.

Farhana, B. (2017). Economic (in)equality and sustainability: preschool children's views of the economic situation of other children in the world. *Early Child Development and Care*, https://doi.org/10.1080/03004430.2017.1372758

Feriver, Ş., Teksöz, G. (Tuncer), Olgan, R., & Reid, A. (2016). Training early childhood teachers for sustainability: Towards a 'learning experience of a different kind'. *Environmental Education Research*, 22(5): 717–746.

Franzén, K. (2015). Being a tour guide or travel companion on the children's knowledge journey. *Early Child Development and Care*, 185(11/12), 1928–1943.

Fujii, O. & Izumi, C. (2008). A silkworm is a fascinating insect for children. In I. Pramling Samuelsson and Y. Kaga (eds), *The contribution of early childhood education to a sustainable society*. Paris: UNESCO, pp. 87–93.

Gandini, L. (2005). *In the Spirit of the Studio: Learning from the atelier of Reggio Emilia*. New York: Teachers College Press.

Georgeson, J. (2018). Sustainable leadership in the Early Years. In V. Huggins and D. Evans (eds), *Early childhood education and care for sustainability: International perspectives*. *TACTYC*. London and New York: Routledge.

Georgeson, J., Campbell-Barr, V., Bakosi, E., Nemes, M., & Pálfi, S., & Sorzio, P. (2015). Can we have an international approach to child-centred early childhood practice? *Early Child Development and Care*, 185(11/12), 1862–1879.

Gunnestad, A., Mørreaunet, S., & Onyango, S. (2015). An international perspective on value learning in the kindergarten – exemplified by the value forgiveness. *Early Child Development and Care*, 185(11/12): 1895–1911.

Gustavsson, L. & Pramling, N. (2014). The educational nature of different ways teachers communicate with children about natural phenomena. *International Journal of Early Years Education*, 22(1), 59–72.

Haddad, L. (2000). *The Ecology of Day Care: Building a Model for an Integrated System of Care and Education*. (Paper presented at the European Conference on Quality in Early Childhood Education.)

Haddad, L. (2006). Integrated policies for early childhood education and care: Challenges, pitfalls and possibilities. *Cadernos de Pesquisa*, 26(129). www.scielo.br/scielo.php?pid=S0100-1574 2006000300002&script=sci_arttext&tlng=en

Haddad, L. (2008). For a specific dignity of ECE: Policy and research issues relating the education of young children and sustainable society. In I. Pramling Samuelsson and Y. Kaga (eds), *The contribution of early childhood education to a sustainable society*. Paris: UNESCO, pp. 36–37.

Haddad, L. (2016). An integrated approach to early childhood education and care and integration within education: The Brazilian experience. *Creative Education*, 7: 278–286.

Halba, H. & McCallum, R. (2011). *Tu Taha Tu Kaha: Transcultural dialogues*. Australasia Drama Studies.

Hall, S. (1992). *The West and the rest: discourse and power in Formations of modernity*. Cambridge: Polity Press.

Harris, K.I. (2015). Developmentally universal practice: Visioning innovative early childhood pedagogy for meeting the needs of diverse learners. *Early Child Development and Care*, 185(11/12), 1880–1893.

Haughton, G. & Hunter, C. (2004). *Sustainable cities*. London and New York: Routledge.

Helavaara Robertson, L., Kinos, J., Barbour, N., Pukk, M., & Rosqvist, L. (2015). Child-initiated pedagogies in Finland, Estonia and England: Exploring young children's views on decisions. *Early Child Development and Care*, 185(11/12), 1815–1827.

Herbert, T. (2008). Eco-intelligent education for a sustainable future life. In I. Pramling Samuelsson and Y. Kaga (eds), *The contribution of early childhood education to a sustainable society*. Paris: UNESCO, pp. 63–66.

Hoffmann, A.M. (2006). *The Capability Approach and educational policies and strategies: Effective life skills education for sustainable development*. Paris: Agence Française du Dévelopement (AFD). Based on three previous papers (presented at the 3rd, 4th and 5th International Conferences on the Capability Approach) on linkages to education as concerns the direct promotion of capabilities through skills-based teaching and learning.

Huggins, V. & Evans, D. (eds). (2018). *Early childhood education and care for sustainability: International perspectives. TACTYC*. London and New York: Routledge.

Isaacs, S. ([1929/1938]2014). *Intellectual growth in young children*. London and New York: Routledge.

Kaga, Y., Bennett, J., & Moss, P. (2010). *Caring and Learning together: A cross-national study on the integration of early childhood care and education within education*. Paris: UNESCO.

Kamara, H.S. (2008). Early childhood education for a sustainable society. In I. Pramling Samuelsson and Y. Kaga (eds), *The contribution of early childhood education to a sustainable society*. Paris: UNESCO, pp. 102–107.

Karlstadt, S.G., Pramling Samuelsson, I., & Broman, I.T (2007). *Early Childhood Education and Learning for Sustainable Development and Citizenship*. Paper presented at 17th EECERA Annual Conference, Prague 2007.

Krechevsky, M., Mardell, B., & Romans, N. (2015). Engaging City Hall: Children as citizens. *The New Educator*, 10(1), 10–20.

Kress, G. (1997). *Before writing: Rethinking the paths to literacy*. London and New York: Routledge.

Levinas, E. (1996). *Etiikka ja äärettömyys*. Keskusteluja Philippe Nemon kanssa. Tampere: Gaudeamus (Ethique et infini).

Levy, D. (2012). Can capitalism survive climate change? *Ephemera Theory & Politics in Organization*, 12(1/2): 253–258.

Linington, V., Excell, L., & Murris, K. (2011). Education for participatory democracy: Grade R perspective. *Perspectives in Education*, 29(1): 936–945.

Luff, P. & Kanyal, M. (2015). Maternal thinking and beyond: Towards a care-full pedagogy for early childhood. *Early Child Development and Care*, 185(11/12): 1748–1761.

Luke, A. (2005). Curriculum, ethics, metanarrative: Teaching and learning beyond the nation. In Y. Nozaki, R. Openshaw, and A. Luke (eds), *Struggles over difference: Curriculum, texts, and pedagogy in the Asia-Pacific*. Albany, NY: SUNY Press, pp.11–25.

MacDonald, M. (2015). Early childhood education and sustainability: A living curriculum. *Childhood Education*, 91(5): 332–341.

Mackey, G. (2012). To know, to decide, to act: The young child's right to participate in action for the environment. *Environmental Education Research*, 18(4): 473–484.

MacNaughton, G. (2000). *Rethinking gender in early childhood education*. London: Sage.

Malaguzzi, L. (1994). Your image of the child: Where teaching begins. *Exchange 3/94*. https://www.reggioalliance.org/downloads/malaguzzi:ccie:1994.pdf

Martlew, J., Stephen, C., & Ellis, J. (2011). Play in the primary school classroom? The experience of teachers supporting children's learning through a new pedagogy. *Early Years*, 31(1): 71–83.

McNichol, H., Davis, J.M., & O'Brien, K.R. (2011). An ecological footprint for an early learning centre: Identifying opportunities for early childhood sustainability education through interdisciplinary research. *Environmental Education Research*, 17(5): 689–704.

Melhuish, E. (2014). The impact of early childhood education and care on improved wellbeing. In '*If you could do one thing . . .*' *Nine local actions to reduce health inequalities*. London: British Academy, pp. 33–43.

Mezirow, J. (1991). *Transformative dimensions of adult learning*. Chichester, UK: Wiley.

Montessori, M. (1946). *Education for a new world*. Madras: Kalakshetra Publications.

Moss, P. (2001). Beyond early childhood education and care. OECD Early Childhood Education and Care conference, Stockholm, 13–15 June, 2001. www.oecd.org/education/school/2535274.pdf

Moss, P. (2007). Bringing politics into the nursery: Early childhood education as a democratic practice. *European Early Childhood Education Research Journal*, 15(1): 5–20.

Moss, P. (2011). Democracy as first practice in early childhood education and care. *Encyclopaedia of early childhood development*. University of London, UK.

Moss, P. & Dahlberg, G. (2008). Beyond quality in early childhood education and care – languages of evaluation. *New Zealand Journal of Teachers' Work*, 5(1): 3–12.

Moss, W.G. (2008). *An age of progress? Clashing twentieth century global forces*. New York: Anthem Press.

Moyles, J. (2001). Passion, paradox and professionalism in early years education. *Early Years: An International Journal of Research and Development*, 21(2): 81–95.

Muehlenhard, C.L. & MacNaughton J.S. (1988). Women's beliefs about women who 'lead men on'. *Journal of Social and Clinical Psychology*, 7(1), 65–79. https://doi.org/10.1521/jscp.1988.7.1.65

Murray, J. (2015). Early childhood pedagogies: Spaces for young children to flourish. *Early Child Development and Care*, 185(11/12): 1715–1732.

NAAEE *Guidelines for Excellence Early Childhood Environmental Education Programs* (2010). For educators, parents, home schoolers, administrators, https://naaee.org/sites/default/files/final_ecee_guidelines_from_chromographics_lo_res.pdf

Neugebauer, R. (2007). Early childhood trends around the world: Twentieth annual status report on for profit child care. *Exchange*, May/June 2007. https://www.childcareexchange.com/library/5017502.pdf

Nganje, W., Schuck E.C., Yantio, D., & Aquach, E. (2001). *Agribusiness & applied economics miscellaneous report no. 190*. Farmer Education and Adoption of Slash and Burn Agriculture Department of Agribusiness and Applied Economics Agricultural Experiment Station North Dakota State University.

Nichols, S. (2007). Children as citizens: Literacies for social participation, *Early Years*, 27(2): 119–130.

OECD *Encouraging Quality in Early Childhood Education and Care* (ECEC) www.oecd.org/education/school/48483409.pdf

OECD *Starting Strong* 2017 www.charlotte-buehler-institut.at/wp-content/uploads/2017/10/Starting-Strong-2017.pdf

Okjong, J. & Stuhmcke, S. (2014). The Project approach in early childhood education for sustainability: Exemplars from Korea and Australia. In J. Davis and S. Elliott (eds), *Research in early childhood education for sustainability: International perspectives and provocations*. London and New York: Routledge, pp. 164–166.

Oliveira-Formosinho, J. & Barros Araújo, S. (2011) Early education for diversity: starting from birth. *European Early Childhood Education Research Journal*, 19(2): 223–235.

Oltermann, P. (2017). Put to the vote: German nursery where children make the decisions. *The Guardian*, 11 August 2017. https://www.theguardian.com/world/2017/aug/11/german-nursery-children-make-decisions-vote-dolli-einstein-haus

Orr, D. (2001). *Loving children: A design problem*. http://designshare.com/research/orr/loving_children.htm

Otieno, L. (2008). Cultural considerations in early childhood education for sustainable development. In I. Pramling Samuelsson and Y. Kaga (eds), *The contribution of early childhood education to a sustainable society*. Paris: UNESCO, pp. 93–98.

Page, J. & Elfer, P. (2013). The emotional complexity of attachment interactions in nursery. *European Early Childhood Education Research Journal*, 21(4): 553–567.

Pearson, E. & Degotardi, S. (2009). Education for sustainable development in early childhood education: A global solution to local concerns? *International Journal of Early Childhood*, 41: 97–111.

Penetito, W. (2009). Place-based education: Catering for curriculum, culture and community. *New Zealand Annual Review of Education*, 18: 5–29.

Pramling Samuelsson, I. & Asplund Carlsson, M. (2008). The playing learning child: Towards a pedagogy of early childhood. *Scandinavian Journal of Educational Research*, 52(6): 623–641.

Pramling Samuelsson, I. & Kaga, Y. (eds). (2008). *The contribution of early childhood education to a sustainable society.* Paris: UNESCO http://unesdoc.unesco.org/images/0015/001593/159355e.pdf

Pramling Samuelsson, I. & Katz, L. (eds). (2008). *The contribution of early childhood education to a sustainable society.* Research Gate. https://www.researchgate.net/publication/265435095_The_Contribution_of_Early_Childhood_Education_to_a_Sustainable_Society

Pramling Samuelsson, I. & Park, E. (2017). *How to educate children for sustainable learning and for a sustainable world. International Journal of Early Childhood*, 49(3): 273.

Prince, C. (2010). Sowing the seeds: Education for sustainability within the early years curriculum. *European Early Childhood Education Research Journal*, 18:3, 423–434.

Qemuge, S. (2008). The role of early childhood education in establishing a sustainable society. In I. Pramling Samuelsson and Y. Kaga (eds), *The contribution of early childhood education to a sustainable society.* Paris: UNESCO, pp. 81–86.

Rana, L. (2017). Globalisation and its implications for early childhood implications. *He Kupu* https://www.hekupu.ac.nz/sites/default/files/2017-11/Globalisation-and-its-implications-for-early-childhood-education.pdf

Reunamo, J. & Suemela, L. (2013). Education for sustainable development in early childhood education in Finland. *Journal of Teacher Education for Sustainability*, 15(2): 91–102.

Rinaldi, C. (2013). Reimagining childhood: The inspiration of Reggio Emilia education principles in South Australia. Adelaide: Government of South Australia. https://www.education.sa.gov.au/sites/g/files/net691/f/reimagining-childhood.pdf

Ritchie, J. (2014). Learning from the wisdom of the elders. In J. Davis and S. Elliott (eds), *Research in early childhood education for sustainability: International perspectives and provocations.* London and New York: Routledge.

Robson, S. & Hargreaves, D.J. (2005). What do early childhood practitioners think about young children's thinking? *European Early Childhood Education Research Journal*, 13(1): 81–96.

Rogoff, B. (1990). *Apprenticeship in thinking.* New York: Oxford University Press.

Rossiter, J. (2016). Scaling up access to quality early education in Ethiopia. Guidance from International Experience. *Young Lives: Policy Paper 8: An international study of childhood poverty.* www.younglives.org.uk

Schumacher, E.F. (1973/1975). *Small is beautiful: Economics as if people mattered.* Perennial Library/Harper & Row.

Scott, W. (1996). Choices in learning. In C. Nutbrown (ed.), *Children's rights and early education.* London: Paul Chapman Publishing, pp. 34–43.

Sen, A. (2000/2013). *The ends and the means of sustainability.* Keynote Address at the International Conference on 'Transition to Sustainability', Tokyo, 15 May 2000. Also in: *Journal of Human Development and Capabilities*, 14(1): 6–20. doi: https://doi.org/10.1080/19452829.2012.747492

Siraj-Blatchford, I. et al. (2002). *Researching effective pedagogy in the early years.* Research report no. 356, Department for Education and Skills, London.

Siraj-Blatchford, J. & Whitebread, D. (2003). *Supporting ICT in the early years.* London: McGraw-Hill.

Siraj-Blatchford, J., Smith, K.C., & Pramling Samuelsson, I. (2010). *Education for sustainable development in the early years.* https://www.gu.se/digitalAssets/1315/1315170_esd-for-early-years---sample.pdf

Skutnabb-Kangas, T. & Cummins, J. (eds). (1988). *Minority education: From shame to struggle.* Bristol: Multilingual Matters.

Smidt, S. (2009). *Introducing Vygotsky.* London and New York: Routledge.

Smidt, S. (2012). *Reading the world: What young children learn from literature.* London: Trentham Books.

Smidt, S. (2013). *Introducing Malaguzzi*. London and New York: Routledge.

Smidt, S. (2014). *Introducing Freire*. London and New York: Routledge.

Smidt, S. (2018). *Introducing Trevarthen*. London and New York: Routledge.

Sommer, D., Pramling Samuelsson, I., & Hundeide, K. (2013). Early childhood care and education: A child perspective paradigm. *European Early Childhood Education Research Journal*, 21(4): 459–475.

Steedman, C. (1987). Prisonhouses. In M. Lawn and G. Grace (eds), *Teachers: The culture and politics of work*. Lewes, UK: Falmer Press, pp. 117–129.

Teise, K.L.G. (unpublished Ph.D. thesis). *Education for sustainable development: Exposing social sustainable policy imperatives for South African education*. University of the Free State.

Tinajero, A. (2010). Scaling up early childhood development in Cuba. Wolfensohn Centre for Development Working Paper no. 16. www.brookings.adu/papers/20/10/04_child_development_cuba_tinajeo.aspx

Tronto, J. (1993). *Moral boundaries: A political argument for an ethic of care*. Hove, UK: Psychology Press.

Tronto, J.C. & Fisher, B. (1990). Toward a feminist theory of caring. In E. Abel and M. Nelson (eds), *Circles of care*. Albany, NY: SUNY Press, pp. 36–54.

UNESCO (2012). Education for sustainable development: Good practices in early childhood. Education for sustainable development in action: Good practices no. 4. Paris: UNESCO. http://unesdoc.unesco.org/images/0021/002174/217413e.pdf

UNICEF (1989). United Nations convention on the rights of the child. London: UNICEF UK, www.unicef.org.uk

United Nations (2015). Sustainable development goals. https://www.un.org/sustainabledevelopment/development-agenda/

Van Keulen, A. & Graaff, F.M. (2008). *Making the road as we go: Parents and professionals as partners managing diversity in early childhood education*. Bernard van Leer Foundation.

Vandenbroeck, M. (2007). Beyond anti-bias education: Changing conceptions of diversity and equity in European early childhood education. *European Early Childhood Education Research Journal*, 15(1): 21–35.

Vandenbroeck, M., Van Laere, K., & Peeters, J. (2012). The education and care divide: The role of the early childhood workforce in 15 European countries. *European Journal of Education*, 47(4): 527–541.

Vecchi, V. (2010). *Art and creativity in Reggio Emilia: Exploring the role and potential of ateliers in early childhood education*. London and New York: Routledge.

Wallis, N. (2017). *Young children, public spaces and democracy: The BRIC Project* https://www.museums.cam.ac.uk/blog/2017/08/10/young-children-public-spaces-and-democracy-the-bric-project/

Wason-Ellam, L. (2010). Children's literature as a springboard to place-based embodied learning. *Environmental Education Research*, 16(3/4): 279–294.

Weldemariam, K., Boyd, D., Hirst, N., Sageider, M., Browder, J., Grogan, L., & Hughes, F. (2017). A critical analysis of concepts associated with sustainability in early childhood curriculum frameworks across five national contexts. *International Journal of Early Childhood*, 49(3): 333–351.

White, E.J. & Redder, B. (2015). Proximity with under two-year-olds in early childhood education: A silent pedagogical encounter. *Early Child Development and Care*, 185(11/12): 1783–1800.

White, J. (2016). *Introducing dialogic pedagogy: Provocations for the early years*. London and New York: Routledge.

Willan, J. (2009). Revisiting Susan Isaacs – A modern educator for the twenty-first century. *International Journal of Early Years Education*, 17(2): 151–165.

Wood, D. J., Bruner, J. S., & Ross, G. (1976). The role of tutoring in problem solving. *Journal of Child Psychiatry and Psychology*, 17(2): 89–100.

Woodhead, M., Bolton, L., Featherstone, I. & Robertson, P. (2014). Early childhood development: Delivering inter-sectoral policies, programmes and services in low resource settings, HEART Topic Guide, Sussex: Health and Education Advice Resources Team (www.heart-resources.org).

Woodrow, C. & Press, F. (2007). (Re)positioning the child in the policy/politics of early childhood. *Educational Philosophy and Theory*, 39(3): 312–325.

Yarrow A. (2015). What we feel and what we do: Emotional capital in early childhood work. *Early Years*, 35(4): 351–365.

Index